CHRIS RYAN'S ULTIMATE SURVIVAL GUIDE

CHRIS RYAN'S ULTIMATE SURVIVAL GUIDE

CHRIS RYAN

CENTURY

Published by Century in 2003

5 7 9 10 8 6 4

Copyright © Chris Ryan 2003

Chris Ryan has asserted his right under the Copyright, Designs and Patents Act,
1988 to be identified as the author of this work

By arrangement with the BBC
The BBC logo is a registerd trademark of the British Broadcasting Corporation and is used under license
BBC Logo © BBC 1996

First published in the United Kingdom in 2003 by Century
The Random House Group Limited
20 Vauxhall Bridge Road, London SW1V 2SA

Random House Australia (Pty) Limited
20 Alfred Street, Milsons Point, Sydney,
New South Wales 2061, Australia

Random House New Zealand Limited
18 Poland Road, Glenfield
Auckland 10, New Zealand

Random House South Africa (Pty) Limited
Endulini, 5a Jubilee Road, Parktown 2193, South Africa

The Random House Group Limited Reg. No. 954009

www.randomhouse.co.uk

A CIP catalogue record for this book is available
from the British Library

Papers used by Random House are
natural, recyclable products made from wood grown in
sustainable forests. The manufacturing processes conform to
the environmental regulations of the country of origin

ISBN 1 8441 3387 7

Illustrations by Brian Robins

Printed and bound in Germany by Appl Druck, Wemding

ACKNOWLEDGEMENTS

Thanks to my agent Barbara Levy, editor Mark Booth, Hannah Black, Charlotte Bush, Ron Beard and the rest of the team at Century.

NOTE FROM THE PUBLISHER

This book is intended as a guide only. The author and publisher expressly do not advocate any activity that could be illegal in any manner. The author and publisher assume no responsibility for any injury and/or damage to persons or property which is incurred as a consequence, directly or indirectly, of the use and application of any of the contents of this work. Nor can they accept any responsibility for any prosecutions or proceedings brought as a result of the use or misuse of any technique described or any loss, injury or damage caused thereby.

In practising or perfecting these survival techniques, the rights of land owners and all relevant laws protecting certain species of animals and plants, and controlling the use of firearms and other weapons must be regarded as paramount.

Traps and trapping. The large deadfall traps featured in this book can be extremely dangerous to humans as well as the prey for which they are intended. Traps with trip wires are easily set off accidentally, so it is important that everyone knows exactly where they are. In survival practice keep people away from them and never leave such a trap set up at the end of an exercise.

FOREWORD

Survival is all about living when events are conspiring to kill you.

As food runs out, water gets short and equipment breaks down, survivors are thrown increasingly back on themselves, and their powers of endurance, know-how and cunning.

A key moment for me, when I walked out of the Iraqi desert over ten years ago, was a hallucination I experienced of my daughter standing in front of me. I was pretty far gone by that stage —a combination of dehydration and exhaustion meant I was blacking out at intervals — and no training manual or exercise had prepared me for the state I was in. Equally, no one had told me I would be saved by an image of my daughter walking in front of me.

Fast forward ten years, and I'm surviving in hostile terrain again - but this time the escape and evasion is for television. *Hunting Chris Ryan* pits me against Special Forces, (two US Navy Seals, a British Paratrooper and a British Marine), in three different hostile theatres: arctic, rainforest and African bush.

I'm dropped off in Siberia and the first thing that happens is that the temperature drops from -29C to -46C. The result of this is that after three days I've got frostbite and hypothermia and I'm dying. Not helping matters are the flashbacks to my long walk and a lot of other stuff as well. I'm so far gone that I can't read my GPS device but in spite of all that I'm convinced that the rendezvous point is situated in a gap in the pine forest a mile or so away. I've no real reason to believe this, but I can sense it so strongly that it's like a hallucination. Could this be a re-run of seeing my daughter in the desert? I was rescued by an hallucination then. Why not now?

It's luck really that I was too far gone to act on my conviction, because it was completely wrong. If I had stumbled towards the gap in the pine forest, I would have died.

What's my point? Quite simply this: in this situation, while no one can say what will save you, you owe it to yourself to keep going as long as you can. All you can do is prepare.

I've put all my experience of survival into this book. I know some of you seek out danger while others might come up against it whether they like it or not. But whatever the case, if this books gets one of you out of a scrape – or stops you getting into one in the first place – it's done its job.

Chris Ryan
Herefordshire, 2003

CHAPTER
ONE

DYING IS NOT AN OPTION

SAS TRAINING IS PRACTICAL AND TOUGH. Our attitude has always been that survival means doing whatever you have to do in order to live.

Let's start with an example. A family – a father, mother and one child -- is touring North Africa, and they venture out into the Sahara desert. Their four-wheel drive breaks down in the middle of nowhere and the father decides he's going to walk back to the nearest settlement to get help.

He's gone a long time. The mother gets worried and goes after him with their child. The father meanwhile has realised that he would be better off at the car and manages to retrace his steps, only to find it deserted. In despair, he heads off once again to try and find his wife and child. None of them is ever seen again.

An example like this shows in the starkest possible terms what survival is all about. Skill, strength, stamina … all are important but there is one factor that influences absolutely everything you do: and that's the ability to make the right decision.

Let's start at the beginning. There was a moment when the man said, 'I'm going to get help'. That was a decision. There was a moment when the woman said: 'We're going after him'. That was a decision too. Both were wrong.

The man was wrong because – despite his anxiety – he should have known that his chances of survival were much greater if the group had stuck together. In a survival situation you play a percentage game, and the evidence shows that a search party is more likely to find a car stuck in the desert than a solitary human being. Besides, a car is likely to hold supplies – especially if prepared for a desert crossing. There should be water, some food, and bits you can pillage to make anything from a heliograph to a solar still. Apart from anything else, the car will make a lovely column of black smoke if you set it on fire.

Just as importantly, the man failed to take into account his wife's potential state of mind on being left alone. She would not only be worried sick about her child, but now her husband as well. Eventually this worry made her leave the sanctuary of the vehicle.

The mother was wrong because she failed to take into account the effect of heat on herself and her child. If she went down, the child would not be able to help her. If the child went down, her chances of getting away would be dramatically reduced and her options would stink. She could either stay where she was and die, or go back to the car having achieved nothing and seriously weakening herself.

All this goes to show that making the right decision is of vital importance when it comes to survival. Instead of thinking, *How do I get help?* the right question to ask is, *How do I survive this?* Getting help may well be a factor, but the important thing to remember is that it's just a part of the big question.

Survival often means thinking smart rather than working hard. In other words, it's not simply about how much you know, it's about using that knowledge as effectively as possible.

Let's look at the example above and give it a different slant. Another family is driving across the Sahara and they get bogged down in sand. They're hopelessly stuck, but they know they must stay by the vehicle, so they settle down to wait for help to arrive.

They ration water. They ration supplies. They build themselves a shelter and take the seats out of the vehicle to sit on. They rest during the heat of the day. At night, they build dew traps and a solar still to boost their water supplies by a precious half-litre a day. They also make rescue symbols in the sand that are large enough to be seen from a passing aeroplane. They take the wing mirrors off the vehicle to make heliographs and cut up the carpets for bedding – it gets cold in the desert at night. They tear out some of the ancillary wiring to make a snare and catch a lizard. They cook it, having made a spark by attaching jump-leads to the battery and arcing the ends over tinder made from a scrap of fabric soaked in petrol, then building a fire with some camel dung they've scavenged. And importantly, they've made themselves a signal fire. Knowing that black smoke will show up best against the desert, they make an inventory of all the right flammable stuff.

Eventually, they see an aircraft. They've prepared for this moment, and they use petrol from the tank to set fire to the spare tyre, which they've doused with engine oil. The thick column of black smoke climbs into the sky. The plane sees it. They all wave to show that they are alive. The plane dips its wings in acknowledgement, and they settle down to wait for salvation - which duly comes the next day in the form of a rescue party led by a grizzled old desert hand.

The family are pleased with what they've achieved. They show their rescuers the solar still, the dew traps, the signals, the shelter – everything, in fact.

'I expect you'll want your vehicle back,' the man says.

The husband explains that it's served them well so far, and if it can be winched out of the sand, so much the better.

'It'll need this,' their rescuer says, holding up an ignition key.

'But that's not even the right key,' the man protests.

The old desert hand goes round the vehicle from wheel to wheel, depressing the valve pin of each tyre with the key, letting out the air. Then he starts the engine and drives the car across the soft sand. 'Shame you didn't know that survival trick,' he says.

And here's another version. Before they set out, the family hires a mobile satellite phone. As soon as they get bogged down, they call for help, are told what to do, and drive on.

The point I'm trying to make is this: think smart before you think hard.

In the normal run of events, the decisions we make generally have a small impact on our lives. Do I get off the motorway or stay on it? Do I get this brand of coffee or that brand? Even the big decisions – buying a house or changing jobs – are hardly matters of life or death. But when it comes to survival, the situation is turned on its head. Firstly, *most* of your decisions are going to determine whether you live or die. Secondly, the right decision might go against all your instincts.

How often have we heard the phrase, *Don't just stand there, do something*? Action often gives us a sense of relief – but unless it's the right action you might well live longer by staying put. So while it may seem tedious to spend a day making and setting snares before sitting down to wait, it is probably a far better use of your time and energy than going out and trying to hunt something down. A long day's hunt will be exhausting and your chances of actually catching anything are pretty slim, unless you are exceptionally skilled. By way of contrast, once a snare has been set up, it will carry on working regardless of what you're doing.

Another misconception is caused by the way you feel - which may not have any bearing on the danger you are in. During the making of *Hunting*

Chris Ryan, the worst I felt was when I was in Belize. At night the mozzies bit right through my hammock, while during the day I was plagued by biting flies, maggots, ticks, leeches - not to mention the heat rash and thirst. Yet I was in no danger at all. The real danger was in Siberia, when I curled up in my sleeping bag and went to sleep. The insect bites won't kill you, but the cold will.

Thinking smart can take many forms. I'm always surprised when people go walking in hostile terrain kitted out as if they're on an army exercise – green tent, khaki sleeping bag, dark jacket, etc. I don't want to knock it but it shows a fundamental confusion in their thinking. Soldiering is mostly about not being seen. On the other hand, in 99 per cent of cases surviving depends on being highly visible.

I think people forget that disaster is never more than a few hours away, maybe less, wherever you are in the world. You can go for a Sunday morning walk in the woods, break your leg and die – it happens. The survival mindset is not to stop taking risks, it's to minimize the chances of dying. So when you buy your tent, or your jacket, or your sleeping bag, ask yourself this: If things go wrong, which is more visible: day-glo orange or camouflage green?

In an actual survival situation, thinking smart means making the right decision. But even that is not enough for an extended survival ordeal. In the long term, survival boils down to three main factors: preparation, determination and, ultimately, other people.

PREPARATION

In the SAS, I always split preparation into three different aspects: physical, equipment and mental.

An SAS soldier is supremely fit – they know how important strength and stamina is. But the sort of survival we're talking about in this book is likely to come out of the blue. In any case, you're not likely to want to devote hours a day keeping your body in top condition – though it's something to think about.

Kit really counts. The right equipment will draw the sting from the worst conditions nature can throw at you while the wrong kit can turn a weekend stroll into a fatal nightmare. If you've got a good tent, a supply of food, cooking facilities and a sleeping bag, you can hunker down in an arctic blizzard and emerge none the worse for wear when it's blown itself out. In slightly less testing conditions, your life can be saved by a windproof lighter and a good penknife.

But if I were going to boil it all down into one rule it would be: keep it stupid-simple. Stupid-simple means your kit and your equipment don't have fancy bits that will drop off in the dark and stop them working. It means that everything is tried and tested - but above all, it means that when you're suffering from hypothermia or heat exhaustion or some other by-product of extreme survival, you can make things work. When I was looking at the kit belonging to the Russian Special Forces in *Hunting Chris Ryan*, I was struck by the strength and lack of elaboration of each item. From their leather boots to their fur hats, everything was tried, tested and effective, like their AK47 assault rifles. By way of contrast, my hi-tech plastic boots couldn't breathe and a layer of ice built up inside them, freezing my feet.

Mental preparation breaks down into two areas: knowledge and attitude.

Survival knowledge is an almost inexhaustible subject and no one is going to have the last word on it. What concerns me above all is knowing how to apply that knowledge - and for that there is no substitute for common sense.

For example, common sense should tell you not to chop wood in the darkness: it's too easy for the blade to glance off a branch you haven't seen and bury itself in your thigh. Then again, if the choice were between chopping wood in the dark and dying of cold, I hope you'd chop wood - because the risk of hypothermia in those circumstances is greater than the risk of burying an axe in your thigh.

But more than anything, it's your mental attitude that's going to get you through when the chips are down.

There are two schools of thought on this. One is to keep cheerful and hope that things will get better. But unless you're a very special sort of person, it's nigh impossible to stay cheerful all the time, even in the best of circumstances. To keep that up when things are bad takes enormous amounts of energy. What is more, it leaves you very vulnerable to a massive downer when you cannot sustain your optimism any longer - and that can be fatal.

I take the opposite approach. My motto is, things can always get worse – and it's pulled me out of some really bad situations. Why? Because I believe the essence of survival is facing up to the truth. Only then can you match the measures to the situation in hand.

And the truth is this: in extreme situations you are going to be running out of resources – food, energy, equipment – from the word go. Before you have got yourself saved you may be hungrier, thirstier, sicker and more exhausted than you would have ever believed possible. To kid yourself that things may get better by being optimistic is to let yourself in for disappointment after disappointment – and that really is a downer.

DETERMINATION

So much for preparation, but what about getting through this experience – minute by minute, hour by hour, day by day? I think one word sums it up: *determination*. Reams have been written about morale, optimism and courage, but when your morale has hit rock bottom and you're scared – really scared – of dying, there's only one thing left: determination.

You must apply determination to everything you do. When you're on the march and at the end of your tether, morale might have got you there, but the thing that keeps you putting one foot in front of the other for that last half-mile is simple determination.

At the other end of the scale, optimism and morale aren't going to make you stick to basic rules about camp hygiene. Determination not to let the situation get on top of you and let standards fall is going to keep you healthy for longer – and therefore alive for longer.

You can help yourself stay determined by setting goals. I've always gone for variety to keep myself going with one big goal – to live – and lots of little ones that can vary from building a waterproof shelter to reaching a natural feature on the landscape before having a rest. The key is to relate the little goals to the big one – everything you do should be focused on the aim of surviving longer and longer.

OTHER PEOPLE

In the vast majority of cases, your survival will come down to the heroism, skill and dedication of rescue teams – and a large slice of luck. A few years back, an army platoon on training in Borneo got into big trouble in a deep, remote gorge. Everything went pear-shaped for them, and after a while a full-scale air search and rescue operation was initiated.

It's hard – almost impossible – to search a gorge in a tropical rainforest from the air. Your targets are going to be somewhere down at the bottom of a large trench and between you and them are an awful lot of very thick leaves. The search went on and on without success, so after a few days they put an SAS guy in the helicopter to help. After about ten minutes he looked out of the window and said, 'There they are.' And they were. He had just happened to look down to the right place at the very moment that one of the lost patrol on the ground was looking up. It was the slightest break in the pattern of the leaves, but that was enough to alert him.

That example has it all: dedication, skill and luck. Of course, it didn't do the Regiment's image any harm at all – and to a certain extent the SAS guy's ability to spot a face was down to his training. But if he had not been looking down at that particular spot, or if the helicopter pilot had been steering a degree or two to the left or right, he would never have seen them.

So part of your job, when you are trying to survive, is to think all the time about the people who are out there looking for you, and try and make things as easy for them as possible. The first point to grasp is that however heroic and dedicated rescue teams are, they're not stupid and don't actively want to risk their lives to save yours. So to increase your chances of survival, make it easy for them. Second, they're only human and can't look in all directions at the same time, so whatever you are doing to attract attention, keep it up for as long as possible. Third, make your own luck by devising as many ways as possible to keep going and be seen. A signal fire is great, but symbols on the

think smart before you think hard

17

ground that are visible from the air will work for you all the time.

Ultimately, however much you know, in a drastic situation you are going to have to find your own way to survive. How you manage that is outside the remit of this book – any book in fact. All I hope to do is show that, beyond skill, courage, determination and luck, the one crucial element in survival is you.

CHAPTER TWO

SURVIVAL EQUIPMENT

LET'S BE PRACTICAL HERE. If you were caught by airport security with your typical survival kit, you'd be banged up before your feet touched the ground. You can't travel with so much as a penknife in hand luggage these days, let alone a machete. Many of the chemicals I talk about to make fire have been terrorist staples for decades. You might get away with a Leatherman-type multipurpose tool, but people have had their nail scissors confiscated at check-in, so don't count on it.

Given that, my basic survival kit would comprise a gill net for fishing, because it's light and incredibly effective, a good torch, a windproof lighter, needles and thread, parachute cord (which you can get from camping or climbing shops), water-sterilizing tablets, and some first-aid basics. Condoms have a great many uses – be imaginative. If I was planning to venture into the wilds in a foreign country, I'd buy a knife there – apart from anything else, it would be adapted to local conditions.

LOCAL KNOWLEDGE

Local knowledge is probably the best tool in your survival kit. If people tell you to log your time of departure, and always to let people at the other end of the journey know when to expect your arrival, do it. They know something you don't: namely that if you break down, you may die. If they tell you there's a hurricane coming, shelter where they're sheltering. If there's an avalanche warning, stay off the slopes. Of course it's tempting to pretend you know more about an area or local conditions that people who have lived there all their lives, but it isn't clever. Similarly, if you want to know which of the local plants are edible and which are poisonous, ask.

A BASIC SURVIVAL KIT

To make a good basic survival kit, establish what you are going to need it for and then work backwards.

There are two pieces of basic kit I would not be without: a strong, waterproof watch and an iridium-type satellite phone. They're not much bigger than mobile phones these days and have the same basic features. The advantage is that they are linked to a network of satellites and offer complete global coverage so wherever you are you can call in for assistance. There are a few things to watch though – as yet, they are not waterproof, so keep yours in a sealable plastic bag. You get about two hours talk time off the battery, so to be on the safe side take a back-up with you. Finally, the battery is affected by cold, so in freezing conditions you'll have to find some way of warming them up before calling. (See also the chapter Moving On.)

> " Survival often means thinking smart rather that working hard. In other words, it's not simply about how much you know, it's about using that knowledge as effectively as possible. "

WATER

Purification tablets are highly effective. Potassium permanganate is a good multi-purpose chemical, (which you can buy in a chemist). Use it to sterilize water, make it stronger as an antiseptic, and stronger still to control skin fungi.

Non-lubricated, heavy-duty condoms can be filled with water. Put them in a sock or even a hat to protect them and stop the contents slopping around.

FIRE

Apart from the trusty windproof lighter, a candle will keep a flame going and you can use wax shavings to help get the tinder and kindling burning. A tampon is a good source of tinder.

SHELTER

Parachute cord is strong, light and adaptable. You can use it as it is for lashing, unpick it to make fine threads for fishing or stitching wounds, or twist the strands to carry heavier weights. A wire saw weighs next to nothing but can cut through branches as thick as your leg.

CUTTING

I haven't heard of anyone getting arrested for carrying old-fashioned razor blades.

FOOD

Snares may not be the kindest way of killing animals, but they could keep you alive. Buy two metres of snare wire – I get mine from a country hardware shop. Fish-hooks are so light you can afford to carry a selection with you.

LIGHT

You can get minute survival lights these days, which will help you read a map in the pitch dark.

ROUGHING IT AND SURVIVAL EXERCISES

If you know you are going into the wild and want a good basic kit, make sure it includes the following, as well as the stuff mentioned above.

Mess tin – go for aluminium. The handle should fold inside it.

Small multi-band radio – to let you know if rescue is on its way.

A strong, two-litre water bottle.

Solid fuel tablets – save them for emergencies.

Flashing bicycle lamp – a pulsing light may attract rescuers.

Torch – Maglites seem to have cornered the market. Get something strong, small and waterproof.

Windproof/waterproof matches – save for emergencies.

Marker panel – a fluorescent panel - of any kind - can save your life. It's

A   *multi-band, short wave radio*
B   *satellite mobile phone*
C   *Global Positioning Satellite (GPS) device*
D   *cooking ring with gas cylinder*
E   *hexiblock*
F   *canteen for drinking water*
G   *map in waterproof cover*
H   *Sylva -type compass*
I   *mini torch*
J   *whistle*
K   *mini compass*
L   *flashing bike light*
M   *condom*
N   *tampon*
O   *Maglite-type torch*
P   *parachute cord*
Q   *gill net*
R   *kit, including fishing hooks, fishing weights and snare wire*
S   *fishing line on hand reel*
T   *windproof lighter*
U   *candle*

an acknowledgement that you accept that things can go wrong anytime, anywhere.

Map in a plastic bag – to protect the paper against water.

Flares – ditto.

Survival bag – a big plastic bag will do, (about 6ft by 3ft), although condensation is a problem. Do not put your head inside it – if the carbon dioxide doesn't kill you it will give you a splitting headache. Better to get a metallic foil bag that will double as a marker panel.

Plastic sheeting – this will act as insulation if you wrap yourself up in it, or as groundsheet and a roof for a shelter. Balance flimsiness against weight.

Mirror – heliographing is the most effective way of getting attention.

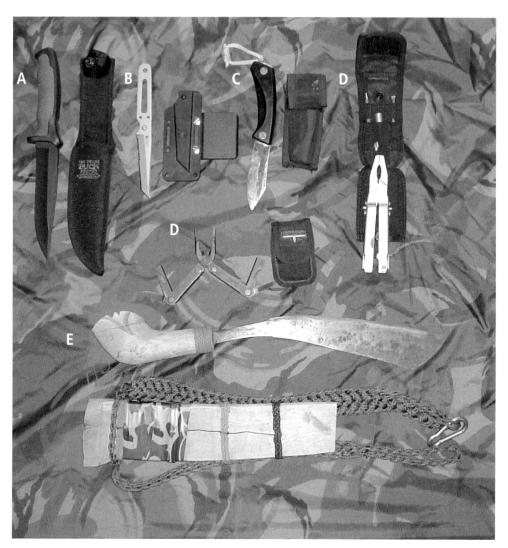

A   *sheath knife and sheath*
B   *serrated knife and sheath*
C   *pocket knife and holder*
D   *Leatherman-type multi-purpose tools (shown open and closed)*
E   *machete and scabbard*

GENERAL EQUIPMENT

When buying anything, whether it's a tent you're looking for or a billycan, go for quality.

KNIVES

Life is a great deal easier if you have a good knife. As there's no point risking it being confiscated at customs, buy one when you get where you're going. Razor blades will do at a pinch but cannot be sharpened and need careful handling. Pocket knives should have a lockable blade and a strong handle. A good sheath knife needs to have:

- a comfortable, wooden handle. It should be a single piece of wood if possible.
- a good blade. You are only as sharp as your knife, as they say.
- a secure scabbard. You want a fastening to hold the knife in the scabbard and a strong loop to hold it on your belt.

FIRST AID

It's no good having a full-blown first-aid kit if you don't know how to use it.

ESSENTIALS ARE:

Plasters – waterproof.

Antihistamines – good for allergies and stings.

Antiseptic – liquid or cream.

Sterile dressings and gauze.

Vaseline – for chafing and chapped skin.

Burn gel

Analgesics – don't use to mask symptoms: your headache might be a warning of dehydration. Reserve for acute pain and bringing down temperatures.

Malaria tablets – the biggest natural killer in the world is the malaria mosquito. Read instructions and follow them. Prepare for possible side-effects. You should note that some courses have to start a while before you expose yourself to risk of malaria.

A FIRST-AID KIT COULD ALSO INCLUDE:

Clips - for sticking the edges of a gaping wound together. Ask at your chemist.

Suturing needles and thread.

Anti-diarrhoea pills – follow instructions.

Antibiotic – some people are allergic to penicillin, so go for tetracycline, (can be found in chemists), and follow dosage instructions.

EMERGENCY RATIONS

In the Regiment we packed what we needed – and what we liked. If we were out for twenty-four hours, some guys would stock up with Mars Bars, others with Kendal mint cake. All thoughts of normal diet went out of the window – we just went for the calories. For anything longer, we'd take a hexamine block for cooking, (a type of slow-burning fire lighter), a billycan and a variety of dehydrated or boil-in-the-bag food.

While dehydrated food is light, clearly there's no point taking it if water is going to be short. Boil-in-the-bag stuff weighs a bit more but you can eat it uncooked.

To a selection of 'main meals' like that, I'd add chocolate or Mars Bars (mint cake if it was hot) and stuff for a brew. Getting something warm in your belly is a morale booster, so take what makes you feel good: tea, coffee, or stock cubes.

> **It's your mental attitude that's going to get you through when the chips are down.**

CHAPTER THREE

GETTING WATER

There are three things that you should bear in mind from the start:

1) You can't survive without water for long in *any* conditions.
2) The more extreme the conditions, hot or cold, the more you need to drink.
3) Everyone will react differently.

In Honduras while I was filming *Hunting Chris Ryan* I kept on the move for an entire day. That evening I sank four litres of water and settled down to sleep, expecting to be in up in the night for a piss. Far from it. In the morning I hardly urinated at all. The next day I cracked on but felt terrible – my head felt like it was split down the middle with an axe and I couldn't really keep my mind on what I was supposed to be doing. That night I drank even more water and it was as well that I did because I was badly dehydrated. One of the hunter force had also come down with serious dehydration and exhaustion and spent a day on a drip in a water-filled hammock.

As well as showing how everyone reacts differently, that's a pretty clear indication of the effects of dehydration on the mind and body.

The reason we've put water first in this section is that it's the basis for all survival and you can never underestimate your need for it. Even if you think you have plenty, always try and replace what you've used whether you are stuck somewhere or on the move.

THE FACTS

Human beings are made up of 70 per cent water. To function on a long-term basis you need to replace the fluids you lose through sweating, urinating and defecating – even breathing. They say that under ideal conditions you should produce about a litre of urine a day.

Water is found in many different types of food – just think how old apples shrink and get wrinkled as the water evaporates from them – but it's unlikely that you'll get enough to survive from moist or pulpy food alone. And you must bear in mind that digesting certain types of food – high protein especially – uses large amounts of your body's fluid resources.

DEHYDRATION

In hot conditions you lose moisture through sweat, which evaporates from your skin. Coldness works differently on the body – it causes stress, stress releases certain hormones, and these hormones cause the body to produce urine. In either condition the blood becomes thicker and stops doing what it should: carrying oxygen to the organs and muscles, and moving heat through the body or out via the skin.

Being dehydrated is very different from feeling thirsty. Thirst is an indication that we need to take on fluids – but when it's used as the only indicator, people tend to take in only two thirds of their daily requirement. Dehydration is a life-threatening condition with its own symptoms. You need to know what these are to prevent dehydration developing into a life-threatening condition.

SYMPTOMS

MILD	MODERATE	SEVERE
Thirst	Very dry mouth	All signs of moderate
Dry lips	Sunken eyes	dehydration
Slightly dry mouth		Rapid, weak pulse
	Skin doesn't bounce	(more than 100 at rest).
	back quickly when	Cold hands and feet
	lightly pinched and	Rapid breathing
	released	Blue lips
		Confusion, lethargy,
		difficult to arouse

WATER NEEDS

It's very difficult to make hard and fast rules about water intake because there are so many variables. Dehydration doesn't depend only on heat: clothing, wind speed, body mass and levels of activity all play a part. What can be measured is ideal water intake according to heat and levels of activity, giving a general indication of how long one can keep going in adverse conditions.

at 15C	litres of water needed per day (approx)
rest in shade	2
light work	3
hard activity	4

at 25C	
rest in shade	4
light work	5
hard activity	6

at 35C	
rest in shade	7.5
light work	10
hard activity	12

at 45C	
rest in shade	12
light work	15.5
hard activity	20

at 50C	
rest in shade	15
light work	20
hard activity	25

If nothing else, the figures shows the enormous impact of heat on water requirement. In a cool climate, your ideal daily water intake if you do eight hours' hard work is between four and six litres. In the desert it is between twenty and twenty-five litres.

In the desert, by doing nothing in the heat of the day you save ten litres of water. That is a massive amount. But think about a real survival situation when you will have nothing like the ideal amount of water. If the ideal is twenty litres and you have only five you are not going to last long at the best of times and your survival time is going to be even shorter if you exert yourself.

Here are some estimated figures for desert survival on limited supplies.

WITH NO WATER

If you try to walk through the heat of the day, you may last no more than four hours. Depending on conditions underfoot, you may travel as little as eight kilometres.

If you rest, you may last for up to two-and-a-half days, maybe longer.

WITH ONE LITRE OF WATER

If you walk at night and rest during the day, you may last two nights and travel anything from twenty to forty kilometres.

If you rest, you could last anything up to a week.

One thing you must factor in is the likelihood that you will be suffering from dehydration from day one and this will affect everything, from your stamina to your ability to think clearly. My advice is to take time at the beginning to sort out priorities, and set some simple goals that you can think of when things get really tough. In Botswana while making *Hunting Chris Ryan* I knew was going to be out for four nights and took four litres of water with me. I covered forty kilometres, three quarters of that by horseback, and by the end I was badly dehydrated with a splitting headache and loss of concentration. The truth is I probably could have looked for well water near habitation but I would not have known whether it was good or not and did not have enough time to purify it – by filtering and boiling or setting up a still of some sort.

PREVENTING DEHYDRATION

If you have any difficulties at all in getting hold of enough water to survive over the long term, the priority is to reduce your water loss to a minimum. Achieving this is about changing habits. For example, in the normal run of things when we're hot we roll up our sleeves to feel the cooling effects of sweat evaporating from the skin. When you're conserving your bodily fluids you keep yourself covered with light fabrics to stop the evaporation. Do as little as possible in the heat of the day. Try and save your exertions for when the worst of the heat has gone. If it's safe, travel at night.

Try and breathe through your nose, so you don't allow your saliva to evaporate. Build a shelter using a double layer of fabric to give you shade and insulation. Cover up with light fabrics if it's really hot. Drink only when the temperature drops. Avoid high-protein foods, which need a lot of water to be digested. Don't drink alcohol, tea or coffee. They make your body produce urine. For the same reason, however thirsty you are, never drink urine or sea water.

In cold weather conditions, where you have to wear layers of clothing, pace your activity to avoid dehydration from sweating. This happened to a mate of mine in the first Gulf War – we were running out of danger, but he hadn't told anyone that he was wearing thermal underwear. Eventually he just blacked out, and we had to rehydrate him.

MAKING WATER SAFE

On day eight, (the final day), of my long walk through the Iraqi desert, I was getting to the end of my tether. I hadn't eaten for a week. I had gone two days straight without water. I was weakened by infections and was having hallucinations. But I still had my two metal water bottles and when I came across what seemed to be a little stream of clear water bubbling out of what looked like a spring, I lost no time in filling my bottles. I had to get right away from the source to drink it and the first sip was a terrible shock. The water was as bitter as acid and burned my lips, mouth and throat. It was clearly poison so I spat it out and poured both bottles away. I found out later that it had been polluted by run-off from a nuclear processing plant.

This tells us something very important about water: however desperate you are, bad water will kill you more quickly than good water. When you're surviving, unless you're really lucky, to drink or not to drink is a dilemma that you will have to face up to every day.

But there are ways of making water safe and you'll need a pretty firm grasp of these if you're going to survive.

There are two stages to making water drinkable: filtering and sterilizing. If the water is clear, you can get away without filtering. If it's cloudy, you must get rid of as much mud and dirt as possible. Impurities will mess up your guts and stop chemical sterilizers from working properly.

FILTERING

Filtering will take out particles of mud, vegetation and some small creatures such as water fleas. You can strain water through fabric — most articles of clothing will do: socks, tights, or anything made of cotton. You can make a simple filter in a hollow tube such as a thick section of bamboo or a plastic bottle with the base cut off. Pack it with layer of grass or moss, then add dry sand or charcoal from a fire. Pour the muddy water in the top and let it drip through. The British Army uses a Millbank bag, (see opposite) — a sort of filter sock that is light and reusable. It's a good bit of kit if you're going to make a habit of surviving.

Commercial pump filters have their advocates but I don't like them much. They do produce clean water but only after an awful lot of work and in hot climates you may end up sweating more water than you're getting.

> **however desperate you are, bad water will kill you more quickly than good water.**

PURIFYING

While particles floating around might be a sign of bad water, the real damage is done by viruses, bacteria and parasites invisible to the naked eye. The only way to get rid of these is by boiling or adding sterilizing chemicals.

STERILIZING

The two main sterilizing chemicals are chlorine and iodine. Always use a good, commercial product — you can pick them up at chemists or camping shops — and follow the instructions carefully. Muddy water needs heavier treatment than clear water, and the colder the water, the longer the chemicals

take to work.

Potassium permanganate crystals are an option. They used to be the traveller's stock disinfectant and can be mixed with other chemicals to make fire (see Chapter 7).

If you're fussy about taste, try dropping a chunk of charcoal into the water after it has been sterilized. After a while, it will absorb some of the chemical taint. If you like to add fruit-flavoured crystals, do not add them with the chemicals. The crystals stop the chemicals working. Wait until you drink before stirring them in.

BOILING

As an alternative to sterilizing, you can boil water vigorously to kill off the bugs. To be on the safe side, make sure it is kept bubbling for three minutes. If you're camping near a ready source of water and have a fire, keep a kettle on the go the whole time. If you can put a lid on the container, so much the better. The water will boil more quickly and you'll lose less through evaporation.

If you're stuck somewhere with lots of fuel, use the boiling method and save the chemicals for when you're on the move.

FINDING WATER

Water flows downhill, so the first place to look for it is in valleys or depressions. If you're lucky, you'll find a fast flowing stream with a rocky bed rising on open land. Walk upstream 100 yards to check for dead animals. If all is clear, go back to your starting point and take water from there.

All animals need to drink, and learning how to read their tracks may help you find where their source of water is. The first thing to do is look for places where animal tracks converge, the second is to watch grazing animals at dawn when they move off to the water hole.

But be careful when you get there: animals have a much higher resistance to water-borne parasites and bacteria than humans. If their watering place is still water, it will be full of life-threatening bugs that they've brought with them. These will give you diarrhoea or worse, and you'll end up losing more water than you take on.

For muddy water holes and rivers, dig a small well two or three metres away and let it fill (see below for more details).

If no surface water is obvious, there may be some just below the ground. Look for vegetation in an otherwise barren landscape then dig a shallow well. Again, we'll go into well types below.

On the seashore, you may find drinkable water behind a line of dunes above sea level. Dig down. If the hole fills, the top couple of inches may be drinkable – fresh water that sits on top of the heavier seawater.

In rocky landscapes, you'll have to rely on natural cisterns where depressions in the rock fill with rainwater. If you come to a cliff-face, examine it carefully for vegetation that may be indicating a natural fissure in the rock with water leaking out of it. If no water is immediately obvious, see if you can squeeze some out of the vegetation, or find a trickle by pulling the greenery and any earth away until you get to the rock face behind it. Cup your hand to trap it, and if you have to lick the rock, go for it. Be patient.

Dew is a source of clean, fresh water that is replenished each morning. You can rub any cotton fabric – a T-shirt for example – on vegetation until it is soaking, then wring it out. If you are on the move, tie absorbent material round your legs to pick up dew as you walk through vegetation. Then take it off and wring it straight into your mouth.

COLLECTING WATER: traps, still and wells

DEW TRAPS

The principle behind the dew trap is the same as steam condensing on a cold bedroom window. However hot and dry it is during the day, moisture will condense on a cold object at night when the conditions are right.

You'll need to scrape out a rounded depression in the ground so that the bottom is a bit deeper than an elbow's depth. Line it with a waterproof material and fill it with stones or boulders, the smoother the better. Overnight, the dew will form and some will pool in the bottom of the trap. You'll need to get to it before sunrise, though, and don't expect much moisture. Dew will also collect on abandoned cars, and you can wipe it off with a cloth, but again, get to it before sun-up. If you clean or dust the metal before the dew forms, you'll get a better drink.

RAIN TRAPS

It's amazing how much rainwater will collect in a trap, so if you're suspending a tarpaulin, make sure it's secure or the weight of water will collapse it. If you leave it on the ground, make sure there's a decent-sized depression for the rain to pool in, and be aware that the rain will probably splash mud into it.

If the soil is right, you can make your own ponds lined with clay. Make as many as you can (not one big one in case it leaks), and cover them over during the day to slow evaporation and stop things falling in.

Always make preparations before it rains so you're not crashing around in the wet.

WELLS

We're not talking about deep wells here, more like holes that fill with water when it's trapped in the soil not too far from the surface. In dried up river beds, water can sometimes be found underground in the outer side of bends.

Dig straight down until you get to wet, water-bearing soil. Then dig a further 30 cm, or about two hand lengths, down. This is so you can collect enough water to make it worthwhile. The first time the well fills, the water will be muddy. Scoop it out and let it fill again. This time it will be clearer.

This is a good way of getting fresh water from around a waterhole or muddy river. If the water looks too filthy or polluted, dig your well further away. If the ground is boggy, a simple well can become a source of water that's free of vegetation. Line it with reeds to strengthen the sides and stop mud getting into it.

> " watch out for insects and snakes and check whether they're edible before getting rid of them "

STILLS

We'll cover two sorts of still: one that uses the heat of the sun and one that uses fire. In both cases the principle is the same: water vapour condenses on a cooler surface and drips into a container. The result is pure, distilled water.

SOLAR STILLS

Dig a round hole – ideally in a dried-up riverbed or anywhere there is likely to be trapped moisture. I recommend about an arm's length

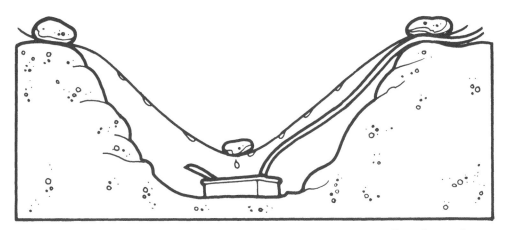

across and an elbow's length deep but its size really depends on how much sheeting you have, and how much digging you can do.

Place a container in the middle of the hole and if you have a long straw or length of tubing, run it from the container to the edge of the hole. Cover the hole with your polythene sheeting – for the hole described above it will have to be two metres square. Anything waterproof will do here, including the flysheet of a tent if you can spare it – but it must be clean. Leave the top end of the tube free.

Next, place a stone in the middle of the sheet, so it dips down and makes an upside down cone *with the deepest point over the container.* As heat builds up under the hole, water trapped in the ground will evaporate, condense on the sheeting, run to its lowest point and drip into the container. You should be able collect about a pint every twenty-four hours without expending any energy but you must move the still every two days.

Because the system produces distilled water, you can moisten the pit with urine or filthy water to help things along.

You'll need to watch out for insects – poisonous and otherwise – and snakes that will be attracted to the shade and moisture. Check whether they're edible before getting rid of them.

A single still will not sustain you over a long period. If you have the resources, dig as many as you can.

FIRE STILLS

Experience shows that these are hard to improvise, and even when you do,

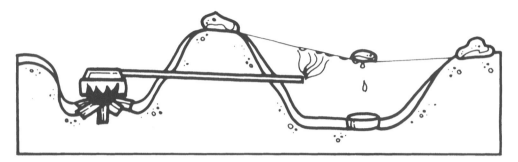

there are four different elements of the apparatus to manage in order to make it work.

1)   the fire
2)   the container for the undrinkable liquid
3)   the condenser
4)   the container for the drinking water

The best container for this is a jerrycan but you could use a saucepan provided you can improvise a top for it.

Make a fire and suspend the container with the undrinkable liquid over it, so that it boils. As you boil the liquid, you want the steam to pass through the tube. During this process it should cool, condense into water and drip into the second container. Try and make the seal for the tube as tight as possible to prevent steam escaping – you want every bit of it to go up the tube.

To help condensation, pass the tube through another container of cool water. If this is impossible, just feed it into the drinking water container and hope that enough condenses in the tube and the container to make the exercise practical.

A plastic bag makes quite a good second container for this method as you can trap the steam in it relatively easily. If you don't have one, trap as much vapour as possible in the second container by using or improvising a lid.

Another possible solution is to dig a pit next to the solar still, have the fire in the bottom of it and run the steam pipe through a hole in the ground into the still, (see diagram). Good luck.

MELT WATER FROM ICE OR SNOW

First thing: just because the weather's freezing, don't forget about dehydration. It's a real threat under all survival conditions, and made much more likely by cold.

Second thing: don't be tempted to suck on icicles or snowballs. In cold climates, your job is to preserve heat. By turning ice to water yourself, you're using up your body's precious reserves of energy, as well as freezing yourself from the inside out.

Ice produces twice as much water as snow for half the heat, so always go for ice first. You may be lucky with icebergs but unless they have come off a glacier, most are just made of frozen sea water which cannot be drunk under any circumstances. As a rule, however, the older the berg the less salty it will be. Bluish ice and weathered contours are signs of age.

THE DIRECT METHOD

Melt snow little by little, until you have hot water in the bottom of your container, then add the rest of the snow bit by bit. If you pack your container with snow, you'll find that the bottom inch or two melts, the water boils away before the heat can melt the snow above and the direct heat damages your cooking equipment.

THE SNOWMAN'S HEAD

Make a tightly packed ball of snow about the size of a snowman's head and secure it just to one side of your fire, perhaps using a pointed stick. See where the water trickles down and put your container underneath to catch the drips. If you put your snowman's head too close to the fire, it may fall in and douse the flames.

THE WATER BAG

If snow is too powdery to pack together, suspend it in a sack made of clothing and place your container under the drips. Again, be careful not to place it too close to the naked flames. You're melting the snow, not trying to boil it.

Lastly, snow may melt if you pack it into a plastic bag, seal it and either keep it around your person or leave on a dark rock in sunlight (dark surfaces absorb heat).

WATER FROM PLANTS

Like all living things, plants need water. While some of them make it available for the survivor, others have learnt the lesson of being too generous and leave nasty surprises to put you off. As a rule, steer clear of plants with milky or coloured sap.

TRANSPIRATION TRAP

Tie a plastic bag around the leafiest bough you can find and make it airtight. As the leaves give off moisture as part of their natural process, water will pool in the bottom corner of the bag. Try not to let the leaves lie too long in the water, as chemicals might leach out of them. Drop a pebble in the bag first so the water pools in the bottom of it, (see above).

PLANTS THAT COLLECT WATER

Some bamboos carry a store of water in their trunks. Usually the older they are the more they have so look for the woody, yellow trunks. Knock them or rock them, listening for a sloshing sound. Then cut a notch at the bottom of each segment to release the water.

Cup-shaped plants often hold water although you should check them for insects, dead or alive.

Bromeliads (Hawaii, southern USA, Latin America, eg pineapples)

Pitcher plants

Traveller's Tree (ravenala madagascariensis)

PLANTS THAT HOLD WATER IN THEIR STEMS

Some vines hold water in their stems and the best way to find out is by trial and error. You have to be careful on two counts.

When you're cutting, watch out for poisonous sap. If it's milky, leave the vine well alone.

Don't put your lips round the vine. Even if the sap isn't poisonous, it might irritate.

The way to get water is to cut a notch in the stem as high as you can, then another lower down. If there's water, it will begin to flow out of the lower notch. Slow it by holding the vine horizontally. Not every vine will produce water, so experiment. Obviously, the thicker the plant the more chance you have of getting a decent drink. Look for ones a couple of inches thick, with rough bark.

TREES THAT GIVE LIQUID

If you cut a banana tree down at knee height and hollow out a depression in the stump, it will fill with water. If the first filling is too sticky and full of tannin, scoop it out and wait for it to fill again.

Fig trees suck up gallons of water at night. You can tap this by cutting an angled notch near the bottom of the trunk, and inserting a V-shaped tube into the notch so that it gets the water but does not tap the tree's milky sap. Angle it to funnel the water into a large container.

Tap coconut, nipa and buri palm trees for a sugary drink by cutting the tip off a flower stem and bending it down. By repeating this every twelve hours you can get up to a quart of liquid a day. Nipa palms have the lowest shoots; you may have to climb for the other two.

Coconuts are filled with milk. Go for the green ones – they are easier to break into and have more milk. To get a drink out of the mature nuts, sharpen a stick and hammer it into the 'eyes', usually found near one end. You can use the husk for tinder and kindling.

Be careful: coconut milk has a laxative effect. If you drink more than three cups a day, you risk losing more liquid through diarrhoea than you're taking on board.

Cacti are tricky. Some are fine to get water from but others protect themselves from predators with poison. The *euphorbia*, which looks like a cactus, is so toxic that people have died eating food cooked on a fire made from it. This is one of those times when you ask the locals for advice.

WATER FROM ANIMALS

Remember, in the long run, you can survive longer without nutrients than without water, and digesting nutrients uses water.

Drinking nutritious liquids such as blood and milk may quench your thirst at the time but will actually dehydrate you over the long term because they need to be digested in your gut. The two sources of water in animals are the eyeballs and the stomachs of grass-eating creatures such as elephants and zebras.

When you're extracting the water from an eyeball, be careful that it doesn't collapse and spill the water. You may want to squeeze it into a container rather than sucking it straight out.

To get liquid from a ruminant's stomach you have to be pretty desperate. Open the stomach sack and pull out the fibrous green stuff you find in it. You'll need to wring the water out of it by squeezing it through a cloth, and then letting it stand to clarify. It tastes foul but it's better than dying of thirst.

Fish carry fresh water in a cavity alongside the backbone. When extracting it, be careful to keep the fish level or it will drain away.

I came across this strange way of finding water and include it as a tribute to mankind's ingenuity and determination. Early in the last century an explorer called Basedow was deep in the outback with his Aborigine guide when the native Australian stopped, dug in the earth and pulled out a large frog. He put the frog's mouth in his and squeezed. To the explorer's surprise, a good half cupful of water came out which the Aborigine drank with relish. So, if you are lost in the Outback, you will pleased to know that *Cyclorana platycephalia* buries itself up 30 cm deep in the earth and keeps a store of drinking water in a specially adapted bladder.

CARRYING WATER

Strong metal water bottles with screw tops can be uncomfortable to carry but are pretty much guaranteed leak-proof. Bladder-type water carriers are more comfortable to transport but can get punctured. Use what's available, but if you have the choice, remember that military equipment is tried and tested in the most extreme conditions.

However, under extreme circumstances use whatever you can. You can improvise with bamboo segments and animal intestines that have been thoroughly cleaned. Condoms are – or should be – leak proof. When filled, put them in a sock to give them a bit of shape and added protection.

CHAPTER FOUR

FINDING FOOD

On tour with the Regiment in the Borneo rainforest, I ate Civet cat. It was horrible – none of the locals would touch it – but easy to catch and nutritious, so down the hatch it went.

By way of contrast, when I was walking out of Iraq, there was simply no time for me to hang around and forage for food. I did the whole, freezing 300km walk in eight days without any food to speak of at all.

Of course there's no comparison between eating the civet and escaping from Iraq – the cat was far worse – but it all goes to prove survival is a question of adapting to every situation as it crops up. In Borneo, I knew I wasn't going anywhere, so it was a worthwhile use of my resources to build and set traps for food. In the Iraqi desert I just wanted to get the hell out of there and my body carried me in spite of what it was put through.

The more you know about finding food in the wild, the safer you will be: you'll expend less energy and run fewer risks of poisoning yourself. Getting food eats up energy and the rule of thumb is not to expend more on getting food than you think you're going to get out of eating it. There's good food and bad food. Bad food isn't likely to kill you outright, it'll just kill you slowly by leaving you too weak to forage. We'll deal with comprehensive food testing later on, but it's important to remember to trust your senses – something we've forgotten about in an era of shrink-wrapped food and sell-by dates. Your body has a strong automatic reaction to bad meats – you retch when you so much as smell it – and that tells you keep away. Plants are trickier to read, but bear in mind that some of the most lethal poisons are taken from plants, so use your common sense: anything that burns you is to be avoided.

Trusting your instincts does *not* mean following your conditioning, and you'll need to discard some preconceptions about what is suitable and what isn't. For example, we think of insects as things to keep out of the house and avoid wherever possible. In many other countries they are seen as a delicious element in a balanced diet. And while the meat-eaters among us might think of a nice juicy steak as a top meal, I would not recommend bringing down a wild ox, butchering it and then eating a slice of its large rump except as a last resort. Apart from anything else, you may find yourself sharing it with other meat-eaters who would see you as a nice meal, not a fellow gourmand.

If you're a vegetarian because you think it's healthy, or simply because you

> **trusting your instincts does not mean following your conditioning**

don't like the taste of meat, hunger and the survival instinct will probably change your tastes and you'll end up eating such meat as you find.

If you're a vegetarian on moral and ethical grounds, my strong advice is to put your ethics and morals aside from day one. You have two responsibilities: to yourself and, if you're in one, to the group.

To refuse meat, when there is meat around, is denying something very basic in your nature: the ability to digest food with and without a face. It's no good refusing meat at first and then taking it when you're in a weakened state. And speaking frankly, I'd have no time for anyone who opted to become a burden on their fellow survivors when they could have avoided it.

SOME BASIC FOOD FACTS

FOOD AS FUEL: CALORIES

The body is a machine that never switches off. Your calorific needs depend on a number of different factors: metabolic rate, physical activity and ambient temperature. Even when resting, you are using up around seventy calories an hour from breathing, brain activity, the heart pumping and the vital organs doing whatever they do. On a lazy day when you don't do much more than potter around, you'll be burning another forty-five calories an hour. If you're working hard, that goes way up and you could be burning 5,500 calories a day. To put it in perspective, an ordinary 500 gm bag of dried pasta has a value of 1,800 calories, so to keep the energy equation equal, you would need to eat three and a bit bags. Except in the wild, you wouldn't just have to eat it. On top of doing everything else – building a hut, trekking up a mountain, swimming a river, foraging – you would have to expend all that energy on making the pasta, assuming you had previously ploughed the field, sown the grain, reaped it and milled it.

In the wild, you will be looking for the foods that give the biggest calorie hit with the least effort. Your gym and your diet are in another world. Put them right out of your head. Keeping an exact balance between the calories you burn and the ones you take on board is going to be very hard. If you're struggling to survive, and using up a lot of calories in the process, it's well nigh impossible. The only thing to remember is never to waste a potential source of food. A handful of berries or a couple of earthworms will keep you alive a little bit longer. And that little bit may be all you need to get rescued.

GETTING THE BALANCE RIGHT: FOOD GROUPS

To stay healthy over the long term, you should try to eat widely and cover as many different food groups as possible. Some shipwrecked sailors starved to death on a diet of wild rabbits – a great source of protein but precious little else. That doesn't mean you shouldn't eat whatever is easily available, it just means that one sort of food is not going to provide a balanced diet. For example, if you're on a seashore and can find a ready supply of eggs, eat them because they are a great source of nutrition. But also think about branching out – remember that seaweeds are edible and catch a bird or some fish (see the following two chapters). The more widely you eat, the more chance you have of getting the balance more or less right.

THE MAIN FOOD GROUPS:

Carbohydrates
Proteins
Fat
Vitamins
Fibre
Minerals

Most things you eat cover a number of different food groups. Meat provides the body with protein but will also contain fats; leafy vegetables provide the body with carbohydrates, but also contain fibre. Vitamins and minerals occur in many different types of food. Meat alone cannot provide all your nutritional needs, but vegetables, if you have the right types in sufficient variety, can. However, when you are surviving you are not going to be in a

55

position to judge whether or not you are getting the right amounts of all the various food groups so the rule is: eat it if you can.

CARBOHYDRATES

Carbohydrates come from plants and are our main source of energy. The body needs them to keep going and so digests them easily. Carbohydrates also help the body break down fat reserves. Without enough carbohydrates, the process is less efficient and produces side-effects: illness accompanied by vomiting and indigestion.

Sugary carbohydrates occur naturally in fruit, syrups, honey and some roots.

Starchy carbohydrates occur naturally in cereals, roots and tubers (eg potatoes). You may have to boil starchy carbohydrates for the body to process them.

PROTEINS

Proteins are the building blocks of life – we need them to build muscles, repair damaged tissue and to grow.

Proteins occur widely. The main sources are meat, fish, eggs and dairy produce.

The main plant sources are nuts, grains, pulses, such as lentils, and fungi. The body can use proteins to generate energy, but only by burning itself up.

FATS

Our society demonizes fat, largely because we get so much of it, but when you are surviving, it is another matter. As the richest source of calories, fat is vitally important during cold weather survival – early pioneers of the polar regions and mountains would take blocks of lard with them to eat. In fact, fat is a form of carbohydrate.

Fat is found in animal meat, fish, eggs, milk, nuts and seeds – think of olive oil and sunflower seed oil. Some vegetables and fungi contain small quantities.

VITAMINS

Vitamins are naturally occurring substances in many foods. Without them, humans fall prey to diseases such as scurvy, beri-beri and pellagra, in anything from a few weeks to many months.

The best sources of vitamins are uncooked fruit and vegetables but the best way to avoid vitamin deficiency is to eat widely.

FIBRE

Strictly speaking, fibre isn't much of a food, but it is vital for your gut to function. Eat fibrous vegetables and whole grains to prevent constipation.

MINERALS

Mineral deficiency is a sign of an unbalanced diet – another reason to eat as many different food types as possible when you are surviving in the wild.

> **slow down, take your time, get a grip and try to keep warm**

WHAT HAPPENS WHEN YOU STARVE

There's a myth that starvation turns you into a sort of instinctive hunter, with acutely sharpened senses and catlike reactions. There may be a short period when you experience a heightened perception of reality, but the truth is that hunger is debilitating, stressful and more likely to result in a downward spiral of inertia.

That's the downside. The upside is that humans, like all animals, have evolved to survive for astonishing periods of time without food, or on a scanty diet. It may not be pleasant but half the battle is to recognise the symptoms, get on top of them and take control.

Because we digest carbohydrates most easily, they are the first reserves to be used up. This is an ongoing process which speeds up when you're expending energy. You should learn to recognise the signs indicating when you're running low on carbs: headaches, bad temper, poor concentration, self-pity, dithering and shivering.

Under normal circumstances, you'd automatically grab a bite to eat. When surviving, you have to respond to what is happening. In other words you are being told to slow down, take your time, get a grip and try to keep warm.

During the next stage your body starts to break down its fat reserves to keep going. A side-effect of this is ketone poisoning. Ketone is a natural by-product that under normal circumstances you would expel in your urine. But if you're really going at it hard and don't have enough to drink, it can build up to dangerous levels and under extreme circumstances put you in a coma. Symptoms range from headaches to vomiting.

After it has got through the fat reserves, your body starts on your protein reserves. The problem is, you are made of proteins – there is about six kilos of the stuff stored in the muscles of an adult male – so when you burn them, your body is effectively eating itself up. It starts on the stomach enzymes – there's no food going in anyway – before going on to the muscles. The result: you get weaker and weaker, pass into a coma and die.

How long all this takes depends on too many factors to make accurate calculation meaningful, such as your fat reserves, your activity levels and the ambient temperature. If you don't exert yourself, stay reasonably warm and have a supply of water, you can survive twenty or thirty days without food.

> **if you don't exert yourself and have a supply of water, you can survive twenty or thirty days without food**

CHAPTER FIVE

PLANTS

PLANTS

There's no way this can be more than an overview of edible plants. Every type of landscape and climate will provide wide variations in what you can find and what you can eat. If you want to find out more, ask around what people eat – and what they don't. When you're foraging for plants, there are certain signs to watch out for that should put you off. Avoid these unless you are absolutely confident about the plant:

most red plants

fruit that comes in five segments

plants with milky sap in the stems

grasses with hooks on stems and leaves

Honourable exceptions include the dandelion, which is edible, and rhubarb, although you should avoid the leaves, which contain oxalic acid.

My advice is to follow local advice if possible, and adopt a *better safe than sorry* approach.

TESTING FOR POISON

You should test every unknown plant to see if it is poisonous.

Test each plant one at a time and don't skip any of the steps. If you suspect that you have been poisoned, drink lots of hot water and try swallowing a bit of charcoal. It may absorb some of the poison and/or help you vomit.

STEP 1

Avoid plants that are old, rotten, worm-eaten or mouldy.

STEP 2

Crush a small bit of the part/parts you are going to eat. If you smell bitter almonds or peaches, it's a sign of poison, so discard.

STEP 3

Rub the crushed plant somewhere sensitive, like your inner wrist. Wait for fifteen minutes and if you feel pain or see a rash, blistering or swelling, discard.

STEP 4

Put the crushed plant in your mouth. DO NOT SWALLOW. If there is any discomfort – such as burning – on the lips, mouth, tongue and especially the throat, discard.

STEP 5

Chew it without swallowing. If it burns, discard.

STEP 6

Chew and swallow a small portion. Wait between five and eight hours without eating or drinking anything else. Watch for sickness, dizziness, tiredness, stomach pains and cramps.

STEP 7

If none of these symptoms occur, eat a handful and wait another eight hours.

STEP 8

Make a careful note of the plant. If it is poisonous you don't want to go through the same process again.

GATHERING

For nutrition, go after roots and tubers, nuts and seeds. Leaves have some nutritional value but are most useful as a source of fibre and vitamins.

ROOTS AND TUBERS

The best time to harvest roots and tubers is in spring, when some of the starch converts to sugar. Cook them first to make them easily digestible. Feel free to cube them, which cuts down the cooking time, but don't peel them as their goodness can lie in or just below the skin. Boiling is easy, but experiment with roasting or baking in hot ashes. When a sharpened stick goes in easily, they are cooked.

IN WATER

Reeds and rushes are often edible and their roots are highly nutritious.

CAT TAIL, GREATER REEDMACE OR BULRUSH TYPHA SPP.

A great source of food, their roots can be easily pulled up. Break them into convenient lengths then bake on embers until charred on the outside. Break them open and eat the insides, spitting out the fibres.

The young shoots are edible raw, boiled or fried. The base of the stem should be boiled, or sliced thin and fried. Steam the young flower heads, and mix the nutritious yellow pollen with water and cook, or add to stews.

FLOWERING RUSH *Butomus umbellatus*

Eat the rootstock after peeling and boiling.

REEDS *Phragmites*

Roasted or boiled, the roots taste sweet. The stem gives off a sweet gum when crushed.

WATER PLANTAIN *Alisma plantago-aquatic*

It grows in mud, and the root needs boiling in two changes of water before eating.

TRUE BULRUSH *Scirpus lacustris*
CLUB RUSH *Scirpus maritimus*

Favouring deep water, these can best be harvested from a boat of some sort. The roots can be roasted.

OTHER WATER PLANTS WITH EDIBLE ROOTS
WATER CHESTNUT *Trapa natans*
Eat the seeds raw or roasted.

ARROWHEADS *Sagittaria*
It's possible to eat the root raw, but cook if possible.

IN FIELDS AND WOODS
BURDOCK *Arctium spp.*
If you collect them in spring they are sweet and so tender they can be eaten raw. Later in the year, roast them in their skins or boil them peeled.

The roots of the dandelion, a relative, can also be eaten when boiled.

WILD PARSNIPS *Pastinaca sativa*
Eat the roots boiled or raw.

PIG NUT *Conopodium majus*
Find the tuber by carefully following the stem under the ground – it is designed to break off to deter hunters. Rub the skin off and eat raw.

COMFREY *Symphytum officinale*
Eat the roots boiled or raw. The starch content is exceptionally high. When mashed, the root will set as hard as plaster.

LESSER CELANDINE *Rannunculus ficaria*
Eat only the tubers after they have been boiled in two changes of water.

SALSIFY *Tragopogon porrifolius*
Cook the roots, eat the leaves.

WILD ONIONS *Allium ursinum*
Add to stews or roast in the embers of your fire. You may have to dig deep to get to these strong-tasting tubers.

THISTLES *Cirsium spp.*
Try and get them young. Roast or boil the root.

KNOTWEED *Polygonum*
The roots can be bitter so soak them before roasting.

SEEDS AND NUTS
Second in importance only to roots and tubers for the survivor, seeds and nuts are a fine source of protein, vitamins and fats. They keep a long time, can be carried easily and should be a priority when foraging.

NUTS
ACORN *Quercus*
Crack the shells by leaving in front of the fire, then boil to remove the bitter tannins, changing the water until it clears. Roast.

PINES *Pinus*
You'll find the pine nut inside the pine cone, which will crack open when heated. Eat them raw or roasted.
SWEET CHESTNUTS *Castanea sativa*

Can be eaten raw but best roasted. Don't confuse with the poisonous horse chestnut, or conker.

HAZELNUTS *Corylus avellana*

Peel and eat immediately as they can go off. Tasty and nutritious.

BEECHNUTS *Fagus sylvatica*

Often overlooked but delicious and nutritious. Heat the seed cases in front of the fire, and peel. Can be eaten raw, roasted or boiled.

WALNUTS *Juglans*

Very nutritious and full of fat. Peel off green outer coating to reveal the more familiar shell.

PISTACHIOS *Pistacia*

Eat raw or roasted.

ALMONDS *Prunus*

Eat raw or roasted but nibble first and discard if bitter. This reveals a build-up of lethal prussic acid.

SEEDS

GRASS SEEDS

Most grass seeds are edible – wheat, oats and barley are types of grass. If you come across a supply, devise a simple container for gathering them. Pull the seed heads off the stem, rub the husks off between your hands and blow the chaff away.

OILY SEEDS

Sunflower seeds are very nutritious, and cracking the shells between your teeth to extract the seed will give you something to do.

With a bit of patience and ingenuity, a car jack can double as an oil press. Wrap the seeds in a cloth, crush and wring out.

FUNGI

Fungi- and that includes mushrooms - can be so dangerous that my advice is to steer well clear of them unless you have real, hands-on experience that includes selecting them, eating them - and living. Do not use this, or any other book, as your sole source of information. Take the time to go out with someone who knows the score and has lived to tell the tale.

POISONOUS FUNGI

There's no food test for fungi – poison fungi can taste as good as safe ones, and the symptoms don't show up for anything up to twelve hours. You have to watch for members of the *Amanita* family, which all share certain characteristics. But others are poisonous too – some of which look like non-poisonous ones – so I advise you to leave both well alone, just in case.

First, follow these basic safety rules:

Don't pick immature mushrooms – you can't tell which are good and which are lethal before they're mature.
Cut away rotten, slimy and worm-eaten bits.
Do not eat anything unless you are 100 per cent sure of its identification.
Cook everything before eating.

Next, follow these basic identification tests, if possible, before picking:

If it has a cup, or volva, at its base poking through the earth, leave it alone.
If it has a scaly ring at its base, leave it alone.
If it has a red cap, red gills, red on the underside of its cap, or red spores, leave it alone.
If it has white gills, white spores or white juices, leave it alone.

IDENTIFYING INDIVIDUAL SPECIES OF POISONOUS FUNGI

In addition to these safeguards, you need to know what each dangerous fungus looks like.

DEATH CAP *Amanita phalloides*
 Greenish cap pale stem, large volva, white gills.

DESTROYING ANGEL *Amanita virosa*
 White all over, large volva, scaly stem, sweet and sickly smell.

FLY AGARIC *Amanita muscaria*
 Bright red cap with white spots.

PANTHER CAP *Amanita pantherina*
 Brown cap with white flecks, white gills.

COMMON EARTHBALL *Scleroderma citrinum*
 Round, leathery appearance. Black inside.

BEECHWOOD SICKENER *Russula mairei*
 Bright red top.

LEADEN ENTOLOMA *Entoloma sinnuatum*
 Greyish white, convex cap, yellow to salmon pink gills, almond smell.

Inocybe *Patouillardii*
 Split cap, white gills that turn olive brown. Bruises red.

Boletus erythropus
 Brownish top, red underneath and on stems.

FALSE CHANTERELLE *Hygrophoropsis aurantiaca*
 Reddish orange, look for gills that run down stem.

Paxilus involutus
 Yellow/brown cap, rolled at edge. Yellow/brown gills that run down to stem.

Cortinarius speciosissimus

Flattish cap and rusty brown gills, can also be confused with the chanterelle.

But the only way to be confident with fungi is to know which ones are safe and stick to them.

EDIBLE MUSHROOMS AND BOLETI

FIELD MUSHROOM *Agaricus campestris*

White, 10 cm cap, dark gills in mature examples.

HORSE MUSHROOM *Agaricus arvensis*

Similar to field mushroom but bigger across the cap.

PARASOL *Lepiota procera*

Plate-sized across the cap, cream gills and scaled cap. Sliding ring on stem.

WOOD MUSHROOM *Agaricus sylvestris*

Similar to horse mushroom, but found in woodland.

SHAGGY INKCAP, Judge's wig

Steeply sloping, cylindrical cap, large white scales with brownish tips. Avoid if scales are dissolving.

PENNY BUN, Cep *Boletus edulis*

Thick, brown 20 cm cap, swollen pale stem.

OTHER FUNGI

BEEFSTEAK FUNGUS *Fistulina hepatica*

Red on top, pink underneath. Old ones are bitter but edible after soaking and stewing.

OYSTER FUNGUS *Pleurotus ostreatus*

Blue-grey, shell-shaped fungus that grows in clumps.

GIANT PUFFBALL *Lycoperdon giantea*

Up to a foot across, choose the white, young ones. Older ones turn yellowish and tough.

TREES

Some people hug trees, but you don't have to stop there. Elephants seek out the Amarula Tree. They eat the fruit which ferments inside their stomach and gets them drunk. I wouldn't recommend this – but there are trees with edible inner bark. Go for the bark low down and never strip it all the way round, as this will kill the tree. Peel off the tough outer layer and strip the inner away with the edge of your knife. It's just about edible raw and in spring can be quite sweet. Otherwise, boil it, let the mass cool, roast it and grind it up for flour or porridge. It's a good source of carbohydrate.

TREES WITH EDIBLE INNER BARK:

Slippery elm
Basswood
Birch
Aspen
Poplar
Maple
Spruce
Willow
Pine

Tree 'tea'

Spruce needles can be eaten when young but at other times of the year strip them from the ends of branches and infuse them in boiling water. This is an important source of vitamin C in cold climates.

Tree sap

Birches and maple have sweet sap that can boiled down to a syrup with a high sugar, and calorific content.

Make a V-shaped cut in the bark. The sap will gather in the bottom of the V, so make a hole under the V and funnel it away from the trunk with a leaf or a piece of wood with a channel carved into it. Let it drip into a container.

KILLER TREES

Don't try and eat from these:

Yew
Cedar
Horse Chestnut
Laburnum
Black locust
Californian laurel
Moosewood
Hickory

FRUIT

Gorging on fruit will probably give you a bad case of the runs. That being said, there is no better source of vitamins. What is more, their strong, clean distinctive taste can act as a real lift when you've been living off scavengings or mush for any length of time.

BRAMBLE

Eat blackberries and raspberries straight from the tree.

ELDERBERRIES

Take them from good-sized trees – the smaller bushes may be a slightly different, yet poisonous, relative. If you eat too many you may throw up, so be careful.

SLOES

Great when added to gin, of course, rather bitter when not. Can be dried and added to stews etc.

ROSE-HIPS

Full of vitamin C, but be careful to extract the actual seeds that can irritate the gut. Split the cases and scoop out the seeds. Drop the cases into boiling water to make rose-hip tea, and when you're finished, eat them.

WILD (CRAB) APPLES

Really bitter and tough when raw, they sweeten and soften up when boiled or baked.

WHITE AND BLACK MULBERRIES

Lucky you.

GRAPES

In the wild these can be bitter but the leaves are edible when boiled.

GREENS

With over 10,000 edible plants in Europe alone, you'd think you were spoilt for choice. The problem is that a great many others are either inedible or poisonous. My advice is to build up a knowledge of the better known edible plants before delving into more exotic species.

We'll start off with some familiar plants before moving onto ones you will need to look for in really challenging environments. Two things to remember:

1. Boiling leaches out nutrients and vitamins so keep the water and drink it.
2. If you're in any doubt, do the edibility test *one plant at a time.*

If you're moving through the landscape, get used to picking plants as you go, either for snacking en route or cooking later.

PLANTS

NETTLES *Urtica spp.*

Go for the young, tender leaves at the top of the stem and boil or add to stews. Cooking de-stings them. Common, nutritious and surprisingly good.

MALLOW *Malva sylvestris*

Leaves are widely used for cooking in other parts of the world.

ROSEBAY WILLOWHERB *Epilobium angustifolium*

Boil or steam the leaves, ditto the young shoots and use the pith from the stem in your stews.

SORREL *Rumex acetosa*

Eat the tips of the young plants. Pleasant, sharp taste.

SEA BEET *Beta vulgaris*

Looks like spinach, tastes like spinach, cooks like spinach.

SEA PURSLANE *Halimione portulacoides*

The fleshy leaves can be steamed or boiled.

SAMPHIRE

Quite a delicacy. Grows in mudflats. Rinse thoroughly before lightly steaming or boiling.

DANDELIONS *Taraxacum*

Pretend the young leaves are wild rocket; boil the older ones. Dandelions will make you urinate, so don't eat if there's a danger of dehydration.

DOCK *Rumex crispus*

Boil the young leaves and change the water if they taste too bitter.

BRACKEN *Pteridium aquilinum*

The upside is that it's common. The downside is that you have to be careful. Eat only the young, curled shoots and only then after you have stripped off the tiny hairs. Boil or roast the roots.

WATERCRESS *Nasturtium officinale*
Look for it in running water. Boil if you think the water is contaminated.

BORAGE *Borago officinalis*
Eat the whole plant, cooked or raw.

ARCTIC PLANTS

You'll find some of the plants listed above growing in colder climates, but few arctic plants thrive in milder climates. Ask around. The harsher the conditions, the further local knowledge will go.

TREES
SPRUCES *Picea mariana, picea rubens*
You can boil the inner bark, and the young shoots at the ends of branches can be eaten raw. Make tea out of the needles for vitamins.

ARCTIC WILLOW *Salix*
You can eat the young shoots, leaves, inner bark and roots when peeled. The leaves are a good source of vitamin C.

BERRIES

CLOUDBERRY *Rubus chamaemorus*

SALMONBERRY *Rubus spectabilis*
Eat the berries raw.

BEARBERRY *Arctostaphylos uvaursi*
Cook berries before eating.

MOSS AND LICHEN

Lichen is a survival food – it is high in nutrients but takes careful preparation owing to its high acid content. After gathering, soak overnight or for several hours in water that you must change before boiling. If you have bicarbonate of soda or a good supply of powdered wood ash, you can boil in a solution to neutralize the acid.

Lichen forms the staple diet of caribou, so can be found in their stomachs, partly digested. Don't be squeamish; this is a great delicacy for some Eskimos.

EDIBLE LICHENS ARE:

ICELAND MOSS *Cetraria islandica*

Looks a bit like seaweed. You may have to boil it, dry it and boil it again before it's palatable.

ROCK TRIPE *Umbillicaria*

You'll have to scrape this from the rock, so rinse it before eating.

REINDEER MOSS *Cladonia rangiferrina*

Arctic lichen that looks as if it has little antlers.

OLD MAN'S BEARD *Lichen alectoria spp, bryoria spp*

It hangs off trees in great festoons and makes good tinder too. Pick through for debris before soaking.

HOT, DRY CLIMATES

Your main priority in hot, dry climates is going to be water, not food. Always bear in mind that digestion will dehydrate you, so do not eat until you are sure you can replace the water you have lost.

However, some of these plants are valuable as a source of liquid in their own right.

DATE PALM *Phoenix dactylifera*

North Africa, Middle East, India. A good indication that water is nearby. The fruit are sweet and delicious, the shoots can be eaten raw, and the young leaves can be eaten after boiling. Tap the trunk for its sweet sap.

MESCAL *Agave*

Africa, Asia, Americas, Caribbean. Boil or roast the stem before flowering.

GOURDS *Cucurbitaceae*

Americas, Africa, Middle East, India. Growing in mats – be prepared to eat almost all the plant: cook the flesh of the fruit, leaves, the seeds (which can also be roasted). Chew the stems to extract water.

ACACIA *Acacia spp.*

Africa, Middle East, Asia and Australia. Boil young leaves and shoots. Seeds are very rich in carbohydrates, fat and protein. Boil, roast or grind into flour. The gum is edible and can soothe internal inflammations.

PRICKLY PEARS *Opuntia*

North America. Go for young fruit. Peel them and eat the insides raw. Roast seeds. Tap stems for water.

BAOBABS *Adansonia*

Africa, Asia, Australia. Eat fruit raw and boil young leaves. Tap the roots for water.

CAROB *Ceratonia siliqua*

Mediterranean, North Africa, Middle East, India. Eat pulp from seed pods. Roast seeds and grind for porridge.

HOT, WET CLIMATES

Tropical climates are abundant in fruit and nutritious plants, but I'm concentrating on the most obvious ones, including the palm family. In almost all palms the growing tip is edible, unless they taste horribly bitter.

The rainforest provides real challenges: the floor is often too dark to sustain much growth and the fruit is high up in the canopy. Look for food along riverbanks, where the sunlight can penetrate, or in natural clearings.

SAGO PALM *Metroxylon*

mostly South-east Asia. This staple of old-fashioned school dinners comers from the spongy, inner pith of the bark.

NIPA PALM *Nipa fruticans*

South-east Asia. The fruit and growing tips are edible and the sap is drinkable.

BANANAS AND PLANTAINS *Musa*

Africa, tropical. Bananas are edible raw, the harder plaintains must be cooked.

SUGAR PALM *Arenga pinnata*

Malaysia and Indonesia.   Tap the trunk for sweet sap.

COCONUT PALM *Cocos nucifera*

Milk is easiest to get from young fruit. Pierce the eyes with sharpened stick and drink straight from the shell. Smash the older nuts open with a rock to get at the white flesh. *Don't* drink too much as it will give you the runs, and *don't* sit down under the tree. A falling coconut can kill you.

PAWPAWS OR PAPAYA *Carica papaya*

Delicious, soothing, moist fruit.

MANGO *Mangifera indica*

Tropical. Look for them in all hot, moist climates.

BREADFRUIT *Artocarpus altilis*

Tropical. Eat raw, but better boiled or roast. Good source of carbohydrates.

GOA BEANS *Psophocarpus*

Tropics. A very amenable plant. Boil the pods and young seeds. Roast the older ones. Eat young leaves raw. The protein-rich roots can be boiled, roast or fried to good effect.

YAM *Pachyrrhizus, Sphenostylis*

Tropics. Boil or roast the tubers.

CASSAVA OR MANIOC *Manihot esculenta*

Tropics. Forms staple diet wherever it grows, the tubers are edible but fatally poisonous unless cooked.

SUGARCANE *Saccharum*

Chew stems to extract the sweet juice

BAMBOO *Bambusidae*

Boil or steam the young shoots

MILLET *Panicum, Pennisetum*

Pull out the seeds, grind or pound then use in cooking.

HOT, WET AND NEAR RIVERS

LOTUS *Nelumbium nucifera*

Asia mostly, but also Africa and North America. Boil young leaves and peeled stems

WATER LILY *Nymphaeaceae*

Tropical and sub-tropical. Boil tubers and stems. Seeds are bitter but edible raw.

SEASHORE

Seaweeds are rich in trace elements, vitamins, protein and carbohydrates, although you shouldn't gorge on them – they have the tendency to purge the gut. Limit your intake if water is scarce because: they have a high salt content and benefit from rinsing, and the high protein levels can leave you dehydrated.

The slender, branched seaweed varieties have highish levels of acid, and while not strictly speaking poisonous, will irritate the gut. So if you can, avoid them along with ones that are pulpy or smell.

It's best to take seaweed when young and cut it, rather than tearing the root, or holdfast, from the rock. That way it can regenerate.

SEA LETTUCE *Ulva lactua*
Atlantic and Pacific. Easy to eat and adaptable, sea lettuce can be chopped and eaten raw, dried and added to soups or lightly boiled.

EGG WRACK *Ascophyllum nodosum*
Widespread. Use young fronds for boiling or steaming. Older plants can be used to wrap food in before cooking on heated rocks.

IRISH MOSS, *Carrageen Chondrus crispus; Gigartina stellata*
Atlantic. Full of gelatine, it can be cooked down to a jelly or added to fruit pulp. Can be dried and used later.

LAVER *Porphyra umbilicaulis*
Atlantic and Pacific. The basis of laver bread. Much easier to dry it, add it to soups, or boil and mash.

DULSE *Rhodymenia palmata*
Atlantic and Mediterranean. High protein and vitamin content. Roll it into tubes and let it dry for a sustaining, chewy snack, or boil it.

SWEET OARWEED *Laminaria saccharina*
Widespread. Boil or steam. Sweet and not too tough.

GREEN ALGAE *Enteromorpha intestinalis*
Pale green and common in cooler waters. The whole plant can be eaten raw, dried or powdered.

Above: Naturally occuring form of viagra to use in times of need!

CHAPTER SIX

FOOD

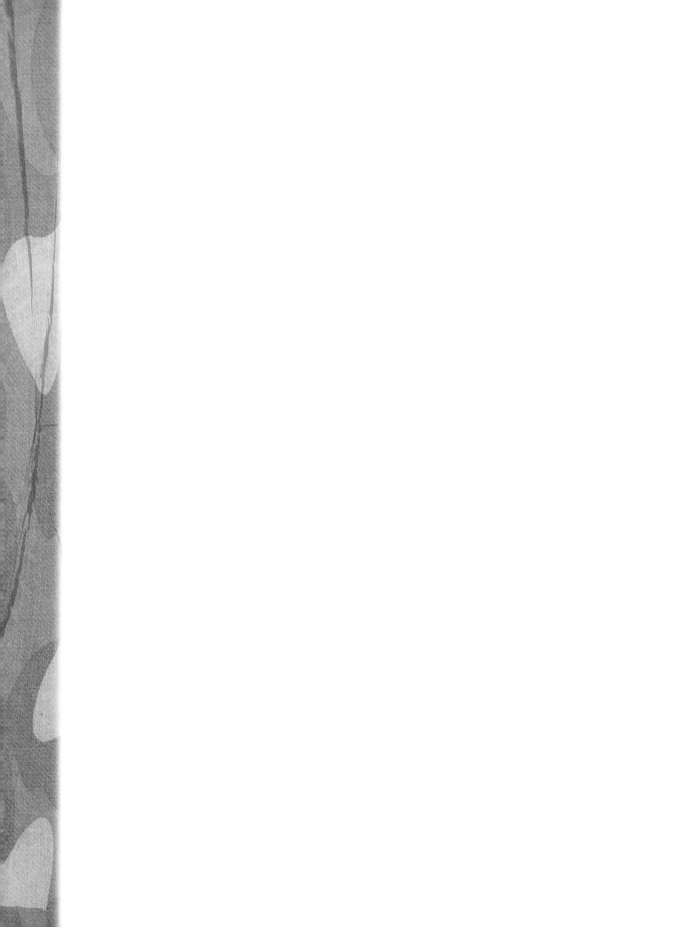

CATCHING ANIMALS

What's the upside to catching and eating meat? It's the best source of protein and fats you'll find in the wild. If it's fresh, it's unlikely to be poisonous. Civet cat apart, it can be uniquely comforting.

Meat does have a downside, however. Animals take great care not to get caught and eaten, so getting hold of meat, whether by trapping or hunting, is labour-intensive. Trapped animals will fight – even a squirrel can inflict a very nasty bite. Some people find killing a dumb animal very hard and butchering it even worse. Vegetarians are used to thinking of meat as a no-go area, and so will have to get over their ideological objections.

And the verdict is? Getting hold of meat in the wild is a challenge but it is one that the human being is pretty well equipped to meet. However fast, strong or cautious an animal is, we have two overwhelming advantages: our brains and our hands. Meat is too good a source of food to ignore in the wild, and if you want to survive you should try to overcome your squeamishness and other objections.

> "however fast, strong or cautious an animal is, we have two overwhelming advantages: our brains and our hands"

ANIMAL TRAPS

When you are surviving, the best way by far to get meat is by trapping and snaring it. While traps and snares do take time to set up, they're working for you the moment you leave them and while you sleep. As such they represent a very efficient use of your energy resources – which is what survival is all about.

I can't stress the importance of starting simply. If something works, use it. There are some pretty elaborate traps described in this section but I would not recommend them until you have got on top of doing straightforward things well.

Because traps are static, the first thing you have to do is work out where the animals are. Many animals follow runs that are visible when you look closely. Small rodents, for example, will patrol an area for food. Foxes are territorial and follow the same paths to and from their dens. Some, like squirrels, will give themselves away by discarding shells at the bottom of trees. Others, burrowing animals for example, will reveal themselves by holes, setts or warrens. However, don't try and catch them too near their dens – they'll be suspicious. Watch where they go and set to work there. With rabbits, you can watch how far they wander, and try and set a snare between them and their warrens. If you panic them, they may well blunder straight into your trap.

The key to trapping is patience. Not all traps work every day or night. Still, if your snare is empty for 48 hours, put it somewhere else.

There's no denying that traps are cruel – especially if you leave an animal in one for a long time. Check them daily – apart from anything else, a trapped animal may attract a predator other than yourself.

For a trap to work it's got to be as unobtrusive as possible. Animals will identify an unfamiliar smell with danger so try to mask your scent if possible, either by wearing gloves or by smearing the trap with something else – herbivore crap is non-threatening and not too vile to handle. Rub recently cut ends of branches with mud, and do the same with the snare if it the wire is glinting.

Finally encourage the animal to run into the snare by placing natural obstacles on either side – the dead branch of a tree or some rocks, for example.

SNARES FOR SMALL GAME

Snares are the easiest traps to set and the easiest snare is a simple loop of wire suspended above a run. The animal puts it head or legs through the loop which tightens like a noose and does not let go.

Killing the animal depends on whether it is a carnivore, and therefore likely to have sharp teeth, or a herbivore, and more likely to be passive. To kill small game, such as a rabbit, hold the neck firmly in one hand and the hind legs firmly in the other. Pull apart across your body with a firm, strong movement until you hear the very clear snap of its neck breaking. To kill a carnivore, sharpen a stick about a foot long and put it through the animal's heart.

MAKING A SIMPLE SNARE

Snares can be made from brass wire, string, hide or nylon, but of all these materials, wire is the best.

You'll need about 80 cm of wire per snare. Make loops at each end, then feed one end through the other. Attach the free end firmly. For a small animal the loop should be a hand's breadth wide and a slightly less than a hand's breadth above the ground.

If you cannot suspend the snare, hold it in place with small forked twigs. A forked twig must also be used to hold the loop open if you are using a string snare.

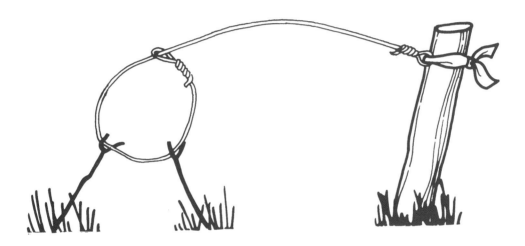

SQUIRREL SNARE

Squirrels are inquisitive, and you can exploit this to trap them. Choose a pole long enough to lean quite high up against the tree; ideally it should reach to just below the foliage and be wedged against the trunk to keep it secure. Attach one or more snares to the pole so that as squirrels run up and down it, they get their heads caught. As one is caught, more may well come to investigate.

THE SPRING SNARE

The disadvantage with the simple snare is that the animal is trapped on the ground and its struggles may work the snare loose from its tether. While losing the animal is an inconvenience, losing a snare could be the difference between surviving and starving. A spring snare is designed to whip the animal off the ground and leave it hanging. As well as making it less likely that you'll lose your snare, other predators will have a hard time stealing your meal.

First select a small sapling near a run. Test it for whippiness. Next, select a piece of wood 20–30 cm long for the upright. Cut a notch in it near one end, and sharpen the other to make it easier to stick into the ground.

The trigger bar needs to be no more than 15 cm long. Notch one end to fit the notch in the upright. Attach it with a cord or wire to the end of the sapling and to the snare. When your prey disturbs the snare, the trigger is released and the animal is yanked off the ground.

There are a number of variations of this trap.

BAITED SPRING SNARE

The second variation of this trap uses a bait. Lay the snare on the ground. Attach the bait to the trigger so that when it is disturbed, the trigger is released and the snare lassoes the prey as it flies up.

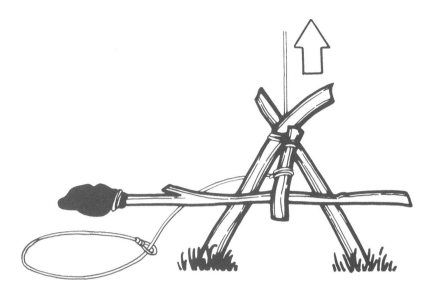

DOUBLE SPRING SNARE

This will work with the sprung sapling or the weighted pole. Select an upright, carve a notch in one end and sharpen the other, as before. Select a trigger bar – this should be thinner than the upright so that it fits across the notch. Hang two snares from the trigger bar and tie a string across each end. Tie this string to another from the pole or the saplings. When the snares are disturbed, the trigger bar is dislodged from the notch and your meal is jerked off the ground.

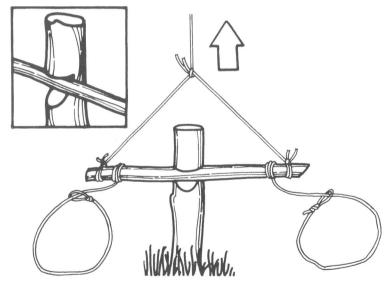

ROLLER SPRING SNARE

The advantage of this method is that it's easy to cover a wide area with it by hanging anything up to a dozen snares from the trigger bar.

Cut a rounded notch in two uprights, sharpen the other ends and put them in the ground on either side of your game trail. Ideally you'll want the game to enter the snare on the opposite side from the notches, so that as it pushes through it dislodges the trigger bar. However, the chances are that it will do this anyway as it struggles.

Make sure the tension on the trigger bar string pulls against the two uprights so that it is kept in place.

SNARES FOR BIGGER GAME

These next snares attract the game with bait. By eating the bait, a trigger is released and the game is caught. Typically this way you will catch small carnivores such as foxes, or a piglet if you're lucky.

BAITED SNARE HOLE

This combination snare and trap will attract animals that dig or disturb the earth to find food. Dig a round hole 10 cm deep and put your bait in the bottom of it. Sharpen four stakes at both ends out of quite whippy wood, such as willow, or hazel, and arrange them evenly around the hole with the sharpened ends pointing down. Anchor the snare above the hole and rest the loop on the sharpened sticks. The animal will push its head past the stakes in order to reach the food, and in so doing will let the snare fall around its neck. When it backs out of the hole, the snare will tighten.

TRAPS

In my opinion, traps can and should be simple affairs that involve the animal falling into a hole, or having something heavy fall on it.

There are more elaborate sprung traps, which often involve firing sharpened stakes, spears or arrows at where you hope to the animal to be. Most of these would do justice to Rambo, and I've included a few — more as a way of illustrating the endless ingenuity of human beings than as a serious means of getting food.

You have to follow certain rules with these. If you are making them recreationally – as an exercise in manual dexterity – they must never be left unattended. The chances of an innocent rambler walking into one and getting killed is too great.

If you are making one in the wild, be very sure that you remember where you have sited it and keep your fingers crossed that you don't end up spearing one of your rescuers.

A quick word about so-called elephant traps – huge holes in the ground with sharpened stakes at the bottom of them. When trying to decide whether or not to build one of these, you should think about possible risks and the calories you are going to burn digging it.

Killing big game this way may work if there are many of you to share the work and the meat. On the other hand, building such a trap on your own will use up valuable calories and the chances are you will only be able to eat a fraction of the meat before it goes off.

As for risks – have you ever tried to kill an angry bear?

TIN CAN TRAP

Bury a tin can on a rodent trail and half fill it with water. Lay grass across it. When small rodents fall in, they won't be able to climb out.

NET TRAP

Set a net at a well-used entrance to a burrow or warren, stop up all the other exits but one and light a smoky fire in it to drive the inhabitants into your trap.

SIMPLE DEAD FALL TRAPS

All these traps work on the same idea: something large and heavy falling on to an animal will kill or disable it.

1 THE TRIPWIRE AND DEAD WEIGHT TRAP

The main components are a tree, a rope, a trigger bar, trigger pegs, an anchor and the weight. Before you do anything make sure of the following:

• you can drill the tree trunk deep enough to take two quite sturdy trigger pegs;

• you are strong enough to lift the dead weight.

Attach the rope to the weight – a tree trunk for example – and lift it using the pulley effect of an overhead branch. Drill two holes for the trigger pegs, angling them so the pegs are pointing slightly downwards. Insert the pegs. Run the rope from the weight, over the branch, down between the pegs where it is held by the trigger bar. Then stretch it across the game trail to the anchor.

There are two things to watch: the pegs must be firm enough to hold the trigger bar in place but short enough to allow it to get dislodged when an animals sets off the trip wire. The rope must be long enough to allow the trunk to fall right onto the ground *or* the jerk of it falling must be strong enough to pull the anchor out of the ground.

When you test it, remember to stay out of the way of the tree trunk and the trip wire which will jerk viciously up.

2. THE BAITED FIGURE 4 TRAP

This looks elaborate but has many advantages: the components are easy to make and pack up small; they can be re-used and it can be adapted to different weights. In other words it's a perfect trap if you're on the move.

It is made of three pieces of wood, all about the same length and thickness – try about 40 cm long and 3-4 cm thick – but it can be made to almost any size. We'll call them the upright, the angle and the baited trigger.

The upright needs to be sharpened at one end (to be dug firmly into the earth) and cut at an angle to the other. Two thirds of the way up, or at the height you want bait to be, cut out a square notch for the baited trigger to rest in.

Cut a notch at one end of the baited trigger, and a square notch half way along, for it to fit into the one in the upright.

Sharpen one end of the angle to fit snugly into the baited trigger's end notch and cut a V-shaped notch in the middle.

The deadfall can be a large, flat rock, a raft of timbers or a net stretched loosely over a frame. It's very effective and worth perfecting. Rest it against the top end of the angle. When the baited trigger is disturbed, it knocks the angle out of the notch and the weight, or net, falls on your prey.

4. THE DEADFALL SCISSORS TRAP

Make this if you have plenty of time. It belongs to the same family as number 1, but it's more accurate. Because of this it is more elaborate. By attracting the animal with bait, and then guiding the weight, you stand a better chance of killing your prey. Also, you can add weights to make the blow even more deadly.

The components are: the dead weight log; at least half a dozen guiding stakes, rope, trigger pegs, trigger.

Before you start lugging heavy logs around, check that you can make the trigger mechanism as outlined above for the tripwire and dead weight trap. Once you have done this, arrange the guiding stakes so that the dead weight will fall on the animal's head and neck when it takes the bait and sets off the trigger. For added effect, pile or tie rocks on top of the dead weight.

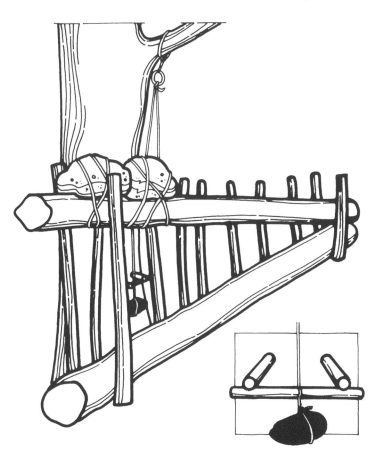

CATCHING BIRDS

Birds will have favourite trees – you look at the ground and on the leaves for droppings. If ever you find a bird's nest with eggs in it, you're in luck. Eggs are nutritious and store well. Eat them raw if you find them while on the move, and if you find a nest while you're laid up somewhere, hard boil or bake them for journeys.

ON THE WING

I wouldn't recommend trying to shoot birds on the wing in any situation where ammunition is limited. If you have a gun, save it for bigger, slower game.

To catch birds on the wing, spend a little bit of time trying to work out their flight paths. Stretch a net between two trees and wait for them to fly into it. To increase your chances, choose trees they feed from. If you don't have a net, try criss-crossing a fishing line in their flight path. Birds flying into it will injure themselves and fall to the ground.

Bats are a delicacy in some parts of the world but bear in mind that they do carry rabies.

ON THE GROUND

All these methods depend on baiting the ground. Take a bit of time for this – in my experience it's often the smaller birds that find the bait first and they attract the bigger ones.

If you've got a clear sweep and are light on your feet, you could try whacking the feeding birds with a long stick or throwing a weighted stick into the middle of the flock and hoping for the best. A trap will however increase your chances of success, and not disturb the rest of the flock so much.

The easiest trap is a container of some sort – a tin would do or even a cardboard box – propped up by a stick. Tie string to the prop and lay the bait. Don't just put it under the trap. Scatter it around and they will get to the trap sooner or later. Conceal yourself, and when a bird takes the bait from the under the trap, pull the prop away. This works best if you keep the string taut – if it's too loose the movement of the string may disturb the bird before the trap falls.

PYRAMID TRAP

You can construct a trap out of sticks made into a pyramid shape. Use the prop and string if you can afford to hang around or improvise with the number 4 trap.

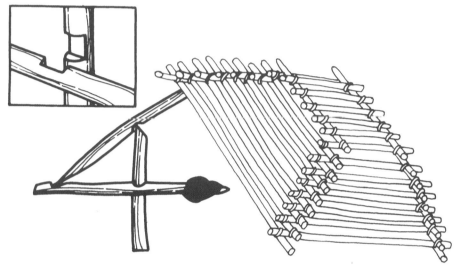

SNARES

You may have luck using snares and bait, though be certain to adapt the loop to the size of the bird. Unless you are in an area where there are a great many ground birds, you'll have better luck with snares on branches where the birds roost.

BAITED HOOK

Birds tend not to be suspicious of what they are eating. For bigger birds such as seagulls, ducks, geese and rooks, a baited fishing hook may well be swallowed whole. I've known seagulls to swallow a baited safety pin swung around in the air. If you're not hanging onto the end, make sure it's well tethered.

A silver diamond-shaped lure – made out of cut metal if possible – pulled through the water or even along a beach may catch a seagull. The lure lodges in its throat and sticks there when you pull.

ON BRANCHES AND PERCHES

Try and work out where birds perch during the day or roost at night. Bird snares do not have to be made of out of wire. Fishing line or string works just as well.

SIMPLE SNARE

The simplest branch trap is a snare suspended above a branch. When a bird feels the snare around its neck, its instinct is to take off forwards, trapping it securely.

SNARED BRANCH

A line of snares tied to a branch or even on a pole secured between two uprights may well catch more than one bird at a time, as they may come to investigate the fluttering bird. You can increase your chances of success by baiting the branch.

LIMING

Make a sticky mixture by boiling holly leaves and starch-rich grain down to a sort of porridge. Spread it on a roosting branch and the birds will stick to it when they land.

ON WATER

HANGING SNARE

A snare suspended from a branch or stretched string above a stream can catch ducks, geese and moorhens.

FLOATING SNARE

See what the ducks are eating, then put this on a float of some sort – a bottle half filled with water or a bit of wood would do. The snare should be held a couple of inches in the air so that the bird puts it head through it to get to the food. Don't forget to anchor the contraption securely to the shore.

BAITED HOOK AND LEAD SLEEVE

A baited hook attached to a float will also catch duck. A good trick is to slide a heavy sleeve on to the line. Keep it in your hand until the bird is caught, then stand up and let the weight slide down to the bird. It will hold the bird's head under water, making it much easier to pull to shore.

SPEAR TRAPS

These are deadly traps designed for deer and pigs and quite capable of killing a human being. If you must use them, remember that animals can't read and put plenty of clear, written warnings all around them.

I would never rely on anything this elaborate but might have a go at making one – if I had time on my hands and degrees in woodwork and engineering.

Short, sharpened stakes can be added to deadfall traps to make them more effective. More elaborate spear traps depend on complex triggers that must be sensitive to being tripped but secure enough to hold the spear in place. Most of them depend on a strong, smooth ring that you carve or make from twine (see section on knots).

When setting these traps, always stand behind them.

TRIPWIRE SPRING TRAP

You will need to position this one on a tree by a game trail. Main components are the spring, the spear, an upright, the slip ring, two trigger sticks and a toggle.

The spring is a shaft of stiff but whippy wood such as yew, hazel, oak, elm or willow. It needs to be a minimum of 100 cm long. Test it by bending it. The spear is a sharp stake about 20 cm long. You'll have to secure this at 90 degrees to one end of the spring shaft, and might want to make a square notch in both components to help them sit tightly together. Lash the spear to the spring, about 15 cm from one end, and then lash the spring to the tree. Make sure that the spear is at the right height for the prey.

Hammer the upright firmly into the ground on the other side of the game trail. Make sure the spring will reach it when bent back.

The more carefully you make the trigger, the better it will work. It can be reused so spend a bit of time on it. The two trigger sticks need to be smooth. Cut one to 20 cm and the other to 15 cm.

Secure the tripwire to the foot of the tree and tie the toggle to one end. The length of the toggle must be greater than the diameter of the ring.

The two trigger sticks are held in place by the ring and the pull of the spring. When the tripwire is disturbed, the toggle releases the trigger and the spear whips down across the path.

HUNTING ANIMALS

Even with a high-powered hunting rifle, it almost impossible to get a kill without stalking the animal first. This takes time, energy and levels of skill that few of us have. Bear that in mind, and ask yourself if you wouldn't perhaps be better off spending the time doing something else: building and setting traps for example, or foraging for plants and vegetables.

There are no hard and fast rules about how close you have to be to an animal – it depends on the animal, the weapon and the conditions. But the purpose of all stalks is to put you as close as possible to your prey for your weapon to have chance a of killing or disabling it.

A successful stalker is able to weigh up a number of variables. Clearly, the more powerful your weapon, the further away you can be from your prey to get a kill and the less chance there is of being spotted. In a real survival situation, however, unless you have the good fortune to be stranded with a high-powered hunting rifle, you are going to have to find of ways of getting as close as possible to your prey without scaring it off.

So as well as staying invisible, the hunter has to know when to stop stalking and start the kill. Only experience can tell you this – few hunters get it right first time, but you can swing the odds towards you by practising both stalking and killing, whenever you can. Improve your chances by not washing with soap, not wearing aftershave and not using toothpaste – not a great hardship when you're surviving. Remember, the more you move, the greater the chance of being seen, heard or of transmitting vibrations through the earth.

MOVEMENT

Move steadily, testing the ground ahead with your leading foot and keeping the weight on your back foot.

If you know where your prey is, stay downwind. On hot still days, this means keeping uphill from them. If you are downhill, the hot air will carry your scent to them as it rises. Make it a general rule to start your hunt early in the day and begin by moving uphill. As the day gets hotter and you prepare to return to your camp, your scent will be carried away from any game in your path.

If you think an animal has seen you, freeze. It is possible they have reacted to movement, and by staying absolutely still you reassure them.

Most animals will smell you long before you smell them – if you smell them at all. Smoke on your clothes and skin can mask your human scent quite well. If you have been in an area for a while, the local fauna will get accustomed to the smoke from your fire and not associate it with danger.

WEAPONS

You will be limited in this by the materials available. Be prepared to improvise, and when you have improvised, be prepared to practise.

BOW AND ARROW

With patience – especially in forming your arrows – this can be an effective and deadly weapon with a good range. Don't do a Robin Hood and try and make a longbow. You can't really afford to spend two years learning how to use it. For convenience, hunters use relatively short bows, about one and a half arms' lengths long.

MAKING THE STAVE

Chose a length of a hard wood. Yew is the best, but oak and birch work well. So that it pulls smoothly you want it to be free of knots and branches. Divide it into thirds and whittle down the two end-thirds. Ideally the bow should be 5 cm thick in the middle, where it needs to be strongest, and taper down to about 1.5 cm at each end. Try and make your whittling as smooth and as even as possible.

Notch the ends to take the string. Use whatever comes to hand – parachute cord, rawhide strip, tough old nettle stems, dried animal gut. Tie one end securely and make a loop in the other. To string your bow, hold one end down against the earth, bend it, then slip the loop into the notch. You want

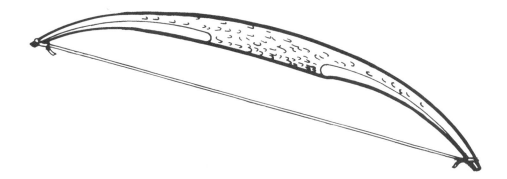

a bit of tension but not too much. Most of the power will come from the pull-back.

To stop the fibres in the wood weakening and the bow-string getting slack, always leave the bow unstrung until you need it.

MAKING THE ARROWS

Arrows need to be straight – the straighter the better. Birch is ideal. Take the bark off and whittle off any lumps and bumps so they they fly smoothly from the bow. How long they are depends on the bow. When the string is pulled back, there should be a couple of inches behind the tip to rest on your stave-hand.

Arrows also need a flight and a sharp tip.

The flight can be made from anything thin and relatively elastic or springy. Card would do, as would thin rubber but feathers are ideal. Split a feather from the thick, bare end. Trim the barbs away from the quill so that a short length of spine is bare at either end. Unlike darts, which have four flights, arrows either have two, on opposite sides of the shaft, or three at four o'clock, eight o'clock and twelve o'clock.

Tie them firmly to shaft by the lengths of spine. Trim the ends of the feathers to make the flights even. Cut a notch slightly wider than the shaft and the flight end.

The tip can be made of anything that carries an edge or a point. It should be heavier than the flights, while the weight will give it stability and penetration. An arrow that flies as close as possible to the horizontal is easier to aim.

You'll want to make the tips in batches and ensure that they are all more

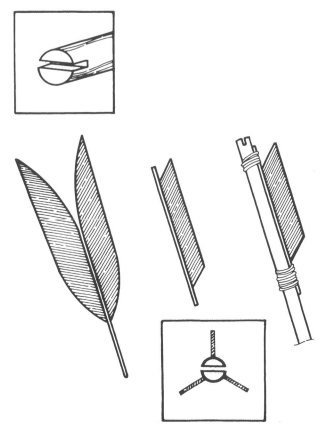

or less the same weight. That means they will all fly in roughly the same way.

If you have any tin cans lying around, cut off the tops and bottoms, squash them flat then cut arrowheads out. Sharpen the leading edges on a stone.

Flint can be turned into arrowheads, and axe heads for that matter, but it takes quite a bit of practice. Start with a bit about the right size and shape, then with another hard rock, chip away at the edges. Flint breaks into sharp planes and with practice good, regular, slightly serrated edges can be formed.

To fix the arrowhead to the arrow shaft, split the end of the shaft, insert the head in it then bind as tightly as possible up to the base of the head itself.

If you have no materials with which to make an arrowhead, select shafts that are slightly heavier at one end than the other – maybe because the wood thickens. Char the end in your fire to harden it, and then sharpen the charred end to a point.

MAKING IT WORK

If you are right-handed, you want to hold the bow in your left hand. A common mistake is to hold the arrow. This makes it hard to control. Hook the index and middle finger of your right hand around the string and hold the arrow in place by squeezing them gently together. Rest the arrow on your left hand and bring the bow up to eye level. Pull the string back, and release the arrow by unhooking your fingers.

If you are doing it right and your bow is strong, a number of things might happen. The arrow will fly out, and the string will snap against the inside wrist of your right arm and possibly graze your cheek. If this is happening, wrap a scarf around your head and protection around your wrist.

CATAPULT

These can be lethal and made from scavenged materials: a forked branch and some inner tube elastic, for example.

BOLAS

Effective against long-legged animals such as deer, the bola wraps a number of its weighted strands around their legs to bring them down. Be sure to follow up quickly with a club or spear to kill your prey before it disentangles itself.

You'll need three to six lengths of twine or string 60 cm long, the same number of roundish stones, along with circles of material to hold them. Adapt the stones to your strength but start off with chicken egg-sized ones.

Wrap the stones in the material and tie the pouch shut, then tie together the other end of the lengths of string. Throw the bola by whirling it around your head two or three times then letting fly. The strands will separate in mid air but wrap around whatever they hit. The bola is highly effective against low flying dense flocks of birds. The more you practise, the better you will get.

PREPARING YOUR MEAT

All meat needs to be prepared before cooking. Blood and innards go off more quickly than muscle or fat, so you need to remove them before they contaminate the whole carcass.

Get into the habit of doing this as quickly as possible after the kill. Don't chuck anything away, even if you can't stand the thought of eating it. Use the bits you don't like for bait.

BIRDS

You can pull small birds' heads off. Larger birds should have their necks broken or their throats cut, although I have seen people press in really hard with their thumbs right on the bird's heart.

Hang it upside down and cut its head off to drain off the blood.

Birds need their feathers and innards removing. Plucking is easiest when the bird is freshly killed. There's no knack to this: put the bird between you legs and pull the feathers out. Keep them for padding, insulation or arrow flights.

If you can't stand the thought of plucking a bird, you can always skin them, although you lose the important nutrients in the skin and the fat immediately below it. Cut the head off, insert your fingers between the flesh and skin and simply pull. The whole skin will come fairly smoothly off the body and legs but stick on the feet, which you then cut off.

To gut a plucked bird, cut off its head, make a cut below its rib cage and pull out its innards and neck bone. The liver, kidneys, neck and heart make a good stock when boiled.

Always boil carrion eaters such as crows and rooks to kill off parasites they have picked up. Try and handle them as little as possible and be extra careful to wash your hands between preparation and eating.

A quick way of getting the breast of a bird is to put a nick in the base of its stomach, hold it by the back legs, hook the first two fingers of your other hand into the nick and locate the breast bone. Then simply tear the breast, bones and all out in one go and pull the meat off. Delicious flash-fried with onions.

ANIMALS

You may have to kill an animal you have trapped. If this is the case, be as quick as you can without putting yourself in danger. No one finds it easy at first – even kittens need to be shown how to kill – but the truth is the less fuss you make about it, the less pain and suffering there will be for the animal, so get used to it.

Even so, some things will take a bit of acclimatizing. If you get a sheep down on the ground and slit its throat, about the last thing it does is lift its head and look you in the eye. Or so it seems.

BIG ANIMALS

A large animal in a trap is a real challenge. Carnivores have teeth and claws; herbivores have vicious kicks. Spear them, aiming for the heart or the neck, where there's a better chance of puncturing one of the main veins or arteries.

You may not kill them outright so when they are weak enough, get in close and club them very hard on the head.

SMALL ANIMALS

Small carnivores, such as foxes or badgers, should be stabbed with an improvised spear – a long, sharp stick will do. Again, be careful – they're fighting for their lives.

Killing small herbivores should be quicker and easier. Kill a rabbit by holding it by the back legs with one hand, round the neck with the other, and pulling. Be firm and confident in what you do. Half-killing an animal because you're sorry for it is no good to man nor beast – literally.

BLEEDING

All animals need a good supply of blood to the head, so the veins and arteries running through the neck tend to be large. To bleed an animal, hang it upside-down from a branch or specially constructed frame. Look for its main vein or artery – this may start to bulge as the blood pools in its head. If not, look for it behind the ears or in the V of the neck. Cutting the throat is effective but messy.

You will want to save the blood if possible, so put a container underneath to catch it.

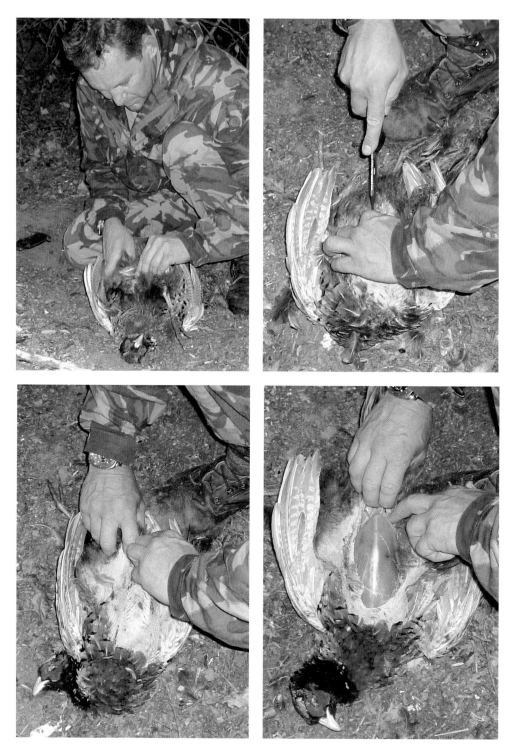

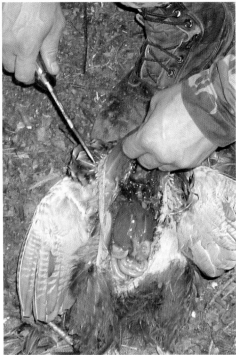

SKINNING ANIMALS

Skinning an animal need not take long. It makes it easier to butcher and you may get a useful hide out of it.

Hanging a large animal up makes skinning it a hundred times easier. Be sure to secure it firmly, either with a rope tied behind its knees or threaded through the tendons above its heels. Like all butchering, a really sharp knife is your friend and less dangerous than a blunt one.

There are two stages to skinning: cutting the skin, and pulling it off. Be careful - you want to try and keep the hide in as good nick as possible. Also, you do not want to risk puncturing the stomach or the intestines – the contents will stink and may contaminate the meat you want to eat. If the animal is properly bled and you follow instructions, skinning is not the messy job it might appear to be.

Don't try to skin a pig – the skin's too tough. Singe the hairs off instead.

CUTTING

Stand facing the underside of the animal. Cut around the back and front legs just above the knee, then cut a circle around the genitals – you want to treat them as part of the gut.

From the knee of each back leg, cut along the inside of the leg to the circle around the genitals. The next cut needs to go from the genitals to the neck. Great care needs to be taken at this stage not to pierce the guts, so go slowly.

Insert your fingers into the cut around the genitals and pull the skin away from the tissue beneath. With the knife pointing down and the cutting edge towards you, very carefully slip it in and bring it down, sawing gently if need be. If you are careful, the guts will be kept in place by the abdominal membrane – and that's where you want them for the time being. Keep your fingers moving behind the knife to lift the skin free.

Cut from the knee of each front leg to the breast, just below the neck.

REMOVING THE SKIN

The trick is to ease the skin off and down. Roll it down the legs. When both are rolled down, cut around the anus and tail. Slide your hands in through the cut you have made in the belly and pull the skin off on one side,

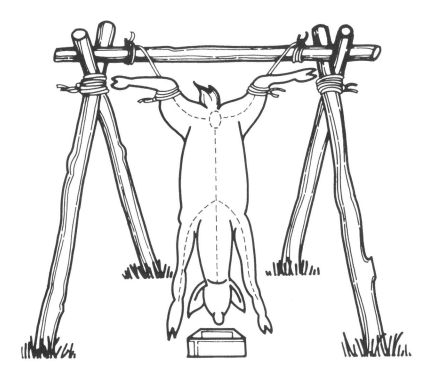

then on the other all the way round to the backbone. Then roll the skin up the front legs, and in theory at any rate you will have a single piece of hide.

SKINNING SMALL ANIMALS

Make a small cut in the belly by inserting the knife into a pinch of loose skin, if possible. Get your thumbs or fingers into the cut and tear outwards. The skin will come away easily.

GUTTING

(See photographs overleaf.) A word of warning – the first time you do this, it seems absolutely revolting. That is no excuse to shirk it, however. Without gutting your animal properly, you run the risk of serious food poisoning.

Lift the membrane from the gut and cut through it carefully. Pull the membrane clear of guts then cut down slowly. The guts will fall out of the cavity and hang there. If you can identify them, cut away the kidneys and liver before they fall on to the ground and get dirty.

When you remove the genitals, make sure you do not pierce the bladder.

FOOD

109

Repeat for the chest membrane and remove the heart, lungs and wind-pipe.

WHAT TO EAT AND WHEN

Just as you have to eat as widely as possible when surviving, so you should never turn up your nose at any edible part of an animal. In the past, people used what they could: from the feet to the ears. You should too – each different type of meat has different qualities and is a source of different nutrients.

Eat the offal first: it is full of nutrients and minerals and goes off quickly.

Liver: check for discolouration and spots. Look in the centre of it for the bile sack and remove. Packed with minerals and vitamins, you can even eat it raw.

Kidneys: eat them and the fat that surrounds them.
Stomach (including contents): tripe, the stomach itself, can be cut into strips and simmered. The partly digested food can be eaten and may have nutritional value. Just try not to think about what you're eating.

Spleen and lungs: don't bother with them.

Pancreas: known as sweetbreads, this can be boiled or roasted.

Intestines: squeeze the crap out them, turn them inside out and wash. They make good sausage skins.

Tail: good stew. Simmer for a long time.

Feet: clean and simmer for a long time.

Head: almost everything can be eaten. Remove the brains and fry them. The head itself can be boiled for the cheeks. Cut out the tongue, boil and skin.

In cool and temperate climates, the carcasses of big beasts will actually benefit from being hung for a day or two. In hot climates you are going to have to eat fresh meat quickly, and then dry or smoke as much as you can.

Don't eat raw polar bear flesh – it's full of really nasty worms that will eat you from the inside out. Avoid its liver altogether, which contains fatal concentrations of vitamin A.

CATCHING FISH

Fishing for survival is different from fishing for sport. Sport fishing involves etiquette and rules to make the process hard. Survival fishing is all about the single-minded pursuit of nourishment and the need to put all resources available to work for you.

NETTING

Stretching a gill net, a light, small-meshed net, across a stream is brutally efficient, so use it and check it every half hour or so.

Because a gill net will catch anything passing through it, you should not leave it down all day in case you end up depleting fish stocks. The best way to keep fish fresh is to keep them alive, so never catch more than you need – unless you are up to salting or smoking them.

TRAPPING

Trapping works by encouraging fish to swim into a narrowing channel and then through the mouth of the trap (see overleaf). Once they are in, they cannot find the trap mouth. Always point traps upstream.

The simplest fish trap is a made from a perspex bottle. Cut the top off just below the shoulder and then push the top back in the other way round. Secure the two halves, weight the trap with pebbles or sand, bait it and wedge it securely in the river or lake.

In a shallow stream, you can make traps that look like fish pens out of sticks or stones. If you find a hollow log, angle sticks around the mouth so that they form a narrowing mouth.

More elaborate traps can be made from flexible twigs – willows are perfect. These are light, fairly portable and endlessly reusable and will earn back more than the time and energy spent making them.

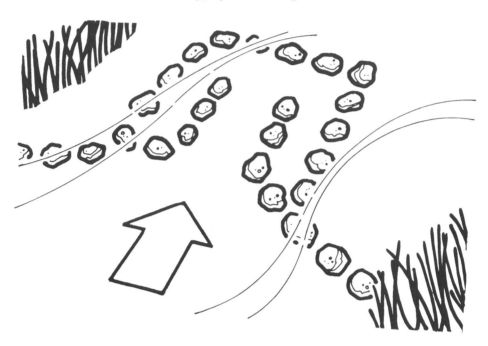

DRIVING

A big group of people linking arms can drive fish onto the shallows where they can be flicked onto the bank. If you scuff up the bottom of a muddy pool or riverbed, the fish will rise to get into the cleaner water.

HOOKING

Fish are not so different from humans. In hot weather they seek out shade and in cold weather they seek out warmth. When it's raining, they tend to stay hidden and they congregate where there's a chance of getting food.

All this means is that fishing can made easier if you bear in mind a few simple pointers as to when and where to catch them.

In hot weather, look for them in shaded parts of the river or deeper parts of a lake. In colder weather, look for them in patches of sunlight or the shallows.

Fish always lie facing upstream so they can see food coming towards them, so you want to let the current carry the bait and hook to them.

In fast-flowing rivers they tend to rest in eddies behind rocks, in the shelter of fallen logs and in slower moving parts of the stream. Insects may fall off overhanging trees or gather at certain parts of the river – perhaps a stretch that is sheltered from the wind. They will also gather where a tributary joins a river: the new stream will wash in food and the churning of the water will oxygenate it.

Fishing can be as labour intensive as you want it, but I've had a lot of success leaving a simple line out overnight that was staked to the bank at one end and weighted to the riverbed at the other.

Fish tend not to feed in the middle of the day, so go for the early morning and late afternoon into night. Spotting fish underwater is a knack /- it's easiest with polarized sunglasses to cut down on glare. The clearest signs that fish are feeding are rings appearing on the water's surface as they rise to take insects.

Remember: while you may not be able to see fish, they will be able to see – and possibly hear – you. They will not feed if they are wary, so tread carefully.

BAIT AND LURES

If you have a ready supply of bait, attract the fish to the area first by scattering it on the water. When they have eaten it safely, they will be more inclined to take it on a hook.

Effective bait: worms, grasshoppers, beetles, small fish, ants eggs. Worms, grasshoppers and beetles will all live for a while in the water, and their struggles will attract fish. Bits of meat may work too. If you have a lot of meat, leave a bit out to attract flies, then use the maggots for bait. If you hang a lump of meat above a good fishing spot, some of the maggots will fall out of their own accord and attract fish that way.

If you have no bait, remember that big fish eat small fish and something small and silver flashing through the water may get a bite. Make a lure out of tin, if possible, or wood wrapped in foil. If you have nothing like this, try wood, feathers – anything. As soon as you have caught one fish, use its guts for bait.

HOOKS

The hook has to be able to take a bait and be strong enough to catch the fish. You can improvise with pins, carved wood, bone, even long thorns.

RODS

A rod can be any length from about five foot. It takes the line to where you want the hook to lie, and a float and weights adjust it further.

Fish feed at different levels in the water, so be prepared to be flexible and use weights to adjust the depth of the hook.

With no weight the hook will sink and the weight of the line will bring it eventually to lie under the tip of the rod. If you cast properly, a float will hold it a greater distance away.

A small weight attached to the line will still allow the hook to move gently in the current, while sinking it to a slightly lower depth.

A heavy weight will keep the hook still, on or near the river bottom.

HAND LINE

This is a way of fishing without a rod. Anything can be drafted in to be used as a reel – a bottle or can for example. Cast the weighted line and then roll it in to bring it back. Try to feel for the tugs as fish nibble at the hook.

Always wrap the line round something to hold on to. A medium-sized fish exerts quite a pull, and if you're holding the line in your hands you can get serious cuts from the nylon when it pulls. Never wrap the line round your finger.

NIGHTLINE

Set hooks at different heights and weight the line so that the lowest is near the bottom.

ICE FISHING

This sets a number of challenges: getting through the ice, keeping the hole from refreezing, not freezing yourself while waiting for the fish to bite.

Without a special ice drill, cutting through ice is labour intensive. Ice chisels help, but any other method is incredibly laborious. I would rather do anything than shiver by a hole in the ice. Tie your line to a stick with a trimmed, angled offshoot. Put another stick across the hole and hook the offshoot over that. Fill the rest of the hole with pine boughs to stop the ice freezing around the line.

You can leave this overnight – but be sure to mark the hole clearly in case it snows or wind blows drift over the hole.

CATCHING EELS

You don't need hooks to catch eels, and it's always worth setting a couple of eel traps or lines, just in case.

Thread a dozen worms on to a length of wool – you might want to twist or plait a few strands together for strength – and tie the worms into a bundle. This is your bait and hook. Tie the wool to a line and anchor it. You might consider tying it to a whippy branch to absorb some of the eel's strength. When it takes the bait, the eel's teeth become tangled up in the wool which holds it fast.

Another method uses a simple trap that can be a net bag or a sack with small holes cut into the side. In the bag put some really high old meat, some vegetation and enough weight to sink it to the bottom of the water. The eels will bite their way into the sack to get to the meat but not be able to get back out again, and you'll find them nestled up in the vegetation.

For a simple box trap you need a wooden box or any sort of container. Cut a hole in it and hang a very simple flap on the inside – cloth will often do. Bait it and weight it. The eel pushes the flap aside to get into the trap but can't work out how to open it the other way.

PREPARING FISH

In hot weather fish can start to go off in a day – starting with the innards – so it's important to gut them as soon as they are dead. Cut them open from the anal vent to the throat and scoop the innards out with your fingers. Use them for an eel trap.

If the fish has scales, rub them off with your knife, working from tail to head. Try and keep the skin – it's nutritious.

To skin an eel or a catfish, push a spike through its gills and hang it up between two forked stakes. Cut around the head and peel it down. Keep eel skin – it's tough and flexible.

SNAKES, FROGS AND REPTILES

The Special Forces in Indonesia have a special way with snakes. They hold a live snake behind the head, rip a strip of skin all the way round with their teeth, tear the rest off downwards, then eat it raw.

My preferred method is to kill the snake first and make a cut through the skin all the way around it, a couple of centimetres behind the head to avoid the poison glands. Secure it, perhaps by pushing a stick through the body below the head and hanging the stick on two forked supports. Skin it in a downward, peeling movement then slice the skin off the vertebrae.

Skin frogs before eating – the skins can be poisonous.

Gut other reptiles, then char the skin in the fire until it cracks. Boil or roast the flesh.

INSECTS

Insects are a rich source of protein and widely eaten, although you should avoid caterpillars. Remove wings and the hard outer carapace where possible. If you have a problem eating then raw, let them dry out and pound them to form a nutritious base for stews. Simply cooking them quickly – whether roasting or boiling – will make them easier to get down.

Locusts: avoid the red ones

Ants: termites are good. To get ant eggs, dig up a nest and scoop the contents into the middle of a tarpaulin. Fold it over and leave. After an hour, open it up and you'll find that the ants will have gathered all the grubs together in the middle.

Grubs: look for wood-boring grubs in fallen palms and mangroves especially.

Snails and slugs: ideally let them starve for a day or two in case they have been eating something that doesn't agree with you, (purging). If you're starving, eat them raw.

Worms: let them purge first, then cook and use as a dietary supplement.

SEA FOOD

SHELL FISH

Most shellfish are filter feeders, which means that they suck large quantities of seawater into the shell and extract the nutrients. Unfortunately, this means that they tend to store whatever nasties are lurking in the water. In the wilds, this is not likely to be a problem, but anywhere near human habitation you have to be careful of human sewage and red algae when it reaches relatively low levels of concentration.

Eat them as soon as you can after catching them.

Mussels and clams: keep overnight in fresh water. Live mussels will close when tapped. Throw away any that don't react. After cooking, either boiling or in the ashes of the fire, throw away any that don't open.

Limpets: strike hard and fast when they are on the rock, aiming to dislodge them in one go. After cooking, discard the blister and eat the rest, Chewy but good.

Octopus: turn inside out to kill them. Boil.

Crab and lobster: the larger ones can be caught in traps baited with meat or oily fish. If it's a bit high, it helps. If you have a net or any sort of material, lay it down flat and put bait in the middle. When the crab or lobster gets close, yank it out of the water. It's worth patrolling rock pools for small crabs. Look under rocks and in seaweed.

SEALS

In colder climates, seal meat is a prime source of food, much prized for its high fat content.

Although they are ungainly on land, seals are fierce and very strong. At the first sign of danger they'll bolt for the sea and it can turn into a race between you and them. The best plan is to try and cut off one, then club it.

> **insects are a rich source of protein and widely eaten.**

CHAPTER SEVEN

MAKING FIRE

When you're up against the elements, fire is a life-saver. Look at it as the most versatile tool in the whole kit. Nothing comes close to the sheer range or number of uses it can be put to.

A good fire will cook and preserve your food, sterilize water and medical equipment, keep insects at bay, defend you against predators and show rescuers where you are. It will help you harden wood to make weapons or dry your wet clothes. By warming you it will lower your stress levels and stop you burning precious calories just to keep warm. As importantly, it will keep your spirits up and give you something to look at in those long evenings whenever nothing else is happening.

BASIC RULES

To work, a fire needs air, heat and fuel.

You can spend anything up to two hours coaxing a fire into life. If it goes out then, you'll be that much colder, that much hungrier and totally gutted.

THINK ABOUT WHERE YOU ARE SETTING YOUR FIRE

Look up to see where the flames might reach, and all around to make sure that it won't spread by accident and cause a disaster. If necessary, clear the ground and/or make a simple hearth using stones, loose earth or sods. If there's a prevailing wind, use it to help you decide where to set it. If you want the smoke to invade your camp to ward off insects, set it upwind. If you don't, set it downwind.

A FIRE NEEDS SHELTER

Strong winds will make it hard to start and harder to control.

KEEP AN EYE ON DRYING CLOTHES

If they are very wet, this will prevent them from catching fire, but as they dry, the risk increases.

NEVER WARM FROSTBITTEN HANDS AT A FIRE

If your hands are too numb to feel heat, you won't be able to tell when they start to cook.

In a mountain or arctic hut, you must follow certain life-saving conventions.

Replace all the wood you have used; make sure tinder and kindling are to hand and properly dried out; leave matches sticking out of the box so that someone with frostbitten or numb hands can get at them easily. Following these conventions might save someone's life. Ignoring them might kill them.

When surviving, put all thoughts of bonfires out of your mind.

Bonfires are designed to burn up fuel. Survival in the wild is all about conserving resources – firewood and your energy. Build a small fire and use survival techniques outlined later on to make the most of the heat.

GETTING A FIRE STARTED

You need to give yourself every chance of getting your fire started. The more difficult the conditions, the more preparation you must do before you even start thinking of lighting the tinder – so sit down and think about what you need and what you are going to do.

WET SOIL, SNOW OR ICE

Build a platform to light the fire on: logs, branches or stones if you can find them. Don't use porous rock. If water trapped inside boils, the rock can explode. If there's anything to hand, think of improvizing a stove.

MARSH OR SWAMP

You'll need a raised platform here too. If you can find rocks, so much the better (though see above). If not, cut four branches with off-shoots. Trim the offshoots, set the branches in the ground to make a square and run support timbers on the trimmed shoots to make support beams. Build a platform on these, and cover with stones or the driest soil you can find.

HIGH WIND

Control is everything. Wind will scatter your tinder, send sparks everywhere and make it impossible to control the rate at which you get through your fuel.

Prepare your fire in a pit, or build a rock circle to keep the worst of the wind off the fire's base. You'll find the rocks useful for cooking and they will retain their heat for a long time – your own night storage heaters.

THE PROCESS

A fire can make the difference between life and death. That means it has to be treated well. Whether your materials are an oil-soaked rag and a wind-proof lighter, or steel, flint and some powdered fungus, starting a fire must always follow the same stages.

You make a spark. The spark starts lights tinder. The tinder lights kindling. The kindling lights main fuel.

However desperate, never take shortcuts by skipping a stage. The chances are it won't work and you'll quickly run through your key resources: tinder, kindling and patience.

For convenience, you may have to light the tinder at a little distance from the fire. In that case, make a tray for it from bark or a flat piece of wood.

> **However desperate, never take shortcuts by skipping a stage. The chances are it won't work and you'll quickly run through your key resources: tinder, kindling and patience**

You can cup this in your hands to shield the tinder from high wind and rain.

Once the tinder is smoking, blow on it gently to create an ember. Feed the ember to create flames. Feed the flames carefully, starting with small twigs or shavings, and building up. Damp logs may not catch when you start the fire, but as it gets hotter the heat will dry them out.

TINDER

There are two sorts of tinder: natural material and man-made material, sometimes chemical in nature. They need to be treated with respect and stored carefully. Natural tinder must be bone-dry if it is going to ignite from sparks, and so it's worth devising a waterproof container of some sort.

Get into the habit of collecting different types of tinder and experimenting with them so you find the method and materials that suit conditions and your own skills best.

NATURAL TINDER

This is just a beginner's list. When you're in the wild, look around and experiment.

Wood shavings: some wood can be scraped into fine shreds. A feather stick is tinder and kindling combined. Because the bottom 'feathers' come from the inner layers of wood, they're going to be the driest. Feather sticks will not start from a spark but should catch from a match or lighter.

Decayed wood: look for fallen tree branches. Pull off bark and dig out soft, rotten wood. Let it dry, then shred or powder it.

Dried bark: you can pull birch bark off living trees in strips. It's a light, fine material that is perfect for tinder. Roll it up to make a simple taper.

Resin: when conifers are damaged they bleed resin that burns easily and strongly. Scrape it off trunks and mix it with other types of tinder to make it more flammable.

Plants and moss: by its nature, most moss is going to be damp. Dry it thoroughly and crumble it. Look for downy seed heads – not all work directly, but some can be mixed with other forms of tinder such as wood shavings.

Lining from birds' nests: birds tend to choose the softest and finest linings for their nest. This makes for perfect tinder.

Termite mounds: pull off a chunk and crumble it.

Fungus: the best is the inner layer of horse's foot fungus – neolithic man used it. Strip off the top layer with a knife and scrape away the spores underneath. That leaves you with a flattish, leathery tongue that can be scraped with the edge of your knife to produce fine fibres. Alternatively, if you've got a fire going and plenty of time on your hands, simmer the fungus for twenty-four hours, hammer it flat then rub hardwood ash into it until it's dry. This was the basis of a commercial fire-lighting product called amadou.

Other fungi work as well, although they do not produce as much material as horse's foot. The cramp ball, which is hard to find outside the UK, can be used pretty much straight from the ground. Break it open and ignite the core. Once it's going, it burns a bit like charcoal.

MAN-MADE TINDER

You'd be surprised what takes a spark. Again, be prepared to experiment – but be careful.

Petrol: lighting a fire is close, manual work and if the petrol flares or spills, you may end up with burns. Petrol-soaked tinder will take a flame well, but may burn out quickly. Keep your kindling handy.

Petrol vapour can explode, so before you make a spark always move the petrol container away from the area. Never keep petrol in your tent.

Never pour petrol directly on to a fire. The explosion can blow your fire out and do some mischief to yourself. If the wind catches it, you'll have burning petrol flying through the air.

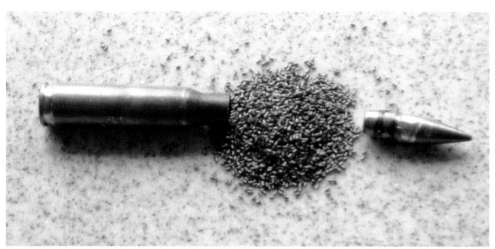

Ammunition: the propellant, what used to be called gunpowder, in shotgun and rifle cartridges burns brilliantly but can go off unexpectedly. It only explodes when in a confined space like a gun barrel but even if you light it in the open it can flare up and burn you.

A rifle round consists of two main parts: the bullet and the metal casing. Hold the casing in one hand, grip the bullet between the finger and thumb of the other, and work it free. It's only designed to go off when you give its base a sharp tap, but be careful and point it away from yourself or the camp.

The propellant is made up of fine, dark granules. Pour it carefully on to your tinder, mix it up a bit and apply the spark.

Shotgun cartridges have a metal cap at one end. (See above.) If you have a knife, cut through the cartridge about a centimetre above the cap, being very careful not to knock it. If you don't have a knife, it's best to go in from the other end. Unpick it and pour away the shots – little round lead ball-bearings. Next you'll find a wad, like a plastic cap. Pull this out. The propellant below it looks like little squares of thin cardboard. Pour it carefully on to your tinder, mix it up a bit and apply the spark.

There is a trick you can do if you're easy with guns or have no other way of making a spark. Remove the bullet or shot, pour out half the propellant, stuff a rag into the top of the cartridge, load it and fire it into the ground. The explosion will light the rag or at least set it smouldering.

Do not be tempted to dismantle larger ordnance – shells and the like. They're too unstable and the propellant is different. If they go off, they'll blow you and your camp to pieces.

Cotton wool and tampons: use the cotton wool as is, but you'll have to unpick the tampons.

Lint: pick away at old bits of rope or fabric you have no use for.

Scorched or charred cloth: this takes a light very easily. The trick is to char the fabric without letting it burn up completely. Hold a piece of natural cloth – cotton or linen – up by a corner and light the bottom corner. Let the flames creep up it then put it out before it has burned up.

Otherwise, pack the cloth tightly into a small tin, make a hole in the lid and put the tin in your fire somewhere you can watch it. When the smoke stops coming out of the hole, the cloth is well and truly charred. Don't forget to let it cool before you open the tin.

Don't bother with fabric taken from inside a car or aeroplane. It's probably been treated with flame-retardant chemicals and you'll have a better chance of getting a wet rock to light.

Film: burns easily, especially when shredded.

MAKING SPARKS AND FLAME

We're going to cover everything in this section, from fire-making techniques used by early man to the latest windproof lighters.

My motto is *If it's there, use it*, so I always take the hi-tech route first. But when you've lost your lighter and your matches are soaked through, you may have to try to make fire the time-honoured way: by bringing two natural materials into contact with each other and creating sparks by percussion or heat by friction.

The first lot of fire-making apparatus to look at is manufactured for that purpose.

LIGHTERS

The best lighters to have in the wild have a piezoelectric system for producing the spark, use liquid butane fuel and burn like miniature blowtorches.

They're reliable and work when damp – although try and get one that has a waterproof top that keeps the workings dry.

Petrol lighters, like the famous Zippo, are strong and reliable, but you can't direct the flame. You can refuel them using ordinary car petrol.

Ordinary gas lighters – the cheap, disposable ones – are better than nothing but have limitations. They go out in any sort of breeze. They won't work if the flint or wheel are wet, and because you light them by flicking the wheel directly with your thumb, any damp on your thumb will knacker them. If that happens, wait for them to dry and start again. If you keep them alight for any length of time, particularly at an angle, the flame melts their plastic casing.

Think of the gas as a precious resource and only use it to light tinder. When they run out of gas, keep them. The wheel and flint can still produce sparks for lighting tinder.

MATCHES

If you know you're going to be stuck out in the wild for any length of time take matches – the more the better. Some people split them in half to make them last longer but it's my belief that this can backfire, so to speak. If the matches are the slightest bit damp the head will crumble and you risk losing a vital match rather than gaining a spare. Better to take twice as many matches.

You can buy specially made waterproof and stormproof matches. Waterproof ones can wear out the striking strip quickly, so be careful. Stormproof matches often just fizz, before lighting the actual match millimetres from your fingers.

Stock up on non-safety matches that can be struck on any rough, dry surface. Keep them dry. When you're on the move, put them in the middle of your pack so that they've less chance of getting wet if there's a downpour, and keep them in a waterproof bag or box if possible – a sponge-bag or a rigid glasses case would do the trick.

If they do get damp, you can dry them using the static electricity in your hair, provided it isn't greasy or damp. Rub them up and down it to create a charge.

If the matches get totally soaked, it's not always possible to save them, but worth a try. Take them out of the box very carefully – you don't want the heads to crumble, and lay them down somewhere warm. If the heads have dissolved and the box is impregnated with the flammable material, dry the box out and cut it into strips for tinder. Save the matches for the same purpose – the traces of chemicals on the head may help them take a spark.

To make matches waterproof, dip them half way down in molten candle-wax. Rub the wax off the heads to strike them.

Preserve your matches whenever possible. If you have a fire going, take a flame from it using a twist of paper or a taper made of bark. If you have any worries about lighting your fire, light a candle with the first match and use that as your source of flame.

If you're tough and want to light matches with your thumbnail, save it for a party trick. White-hot, burning sulphur behind the nail hurts like hell and in tropical conditions will go septic in no time at all.

THINGS THAT MAKE SPARKS

These days camping shops stock a huge range of sparking tools. The basis

of most of these is an alloy that makes a shower of white-hot sparks when struck by anything hard, like a stone or metal. You can buy these as machines, where by spinning wheel makes a shower of sparks, or as a kit with a striking stick and blade, or just a striking stick on its own. Some come attached to a block of magnesium from which you take shavings to set alight with the sparks. Magnesium burns at 5,000C — hot enough to ignite damp tinder.

My advice is to buy a lighter first, and think of these alternatives as back-up. That means going for the simplest option. A good striking stick will last for ages and produce enough sparks to be seen a fair distance away at night — a useful signalling device.

Arrange things so that the shower of sparks has the shortest possible distance to fall on to the tinder. As soon as it has landed, blow gently to encourage the smouldering sparks to ignite.

IMPROVIZED SPARKS

I wouldn't venture out into the wilds without some form of fire-starting kit, but sometimes improvization is the only way. These are some of the commonplace items, man-made and natural, that can be used to get a fire going.

ANTIFREEZE AND STERILIZING CRYSTALS

You'll need potassium permanganate sterilizer crystals for this. Put a teaspoon of them on to something flammable like a sheet of paper or dry cloth. Add a few drops of neat antifreeze then wrap the cloth or paper up around the mixture tightly — it needs this to get the chemical reaction going. Arrange the tinder and/or kindling. Wait a minute. It should ignite on its own as the glycerine in the antifreeze starts a chemical reaction with the potassium permanganate.

SUGAR AND STERILIZING CRYSTALS

Another use for potassium permanganate. Mix nine units of potassium permanganate with one unit of sugar. Make sparks by hitting it or rubbing it between two stones.

THROAT LOZENGES, SUGAR AND CAR BATTERY ACID

This only works with throat pills that use potassium chlorate as an active ingredient. Crush the tablets – you'll need a ratio of three units of potassium chlorate to one of sugar, so experiment with quantities. For spontaneous combustion, let a few drops of sulphuric acid – found in car batteries – fall into this mixture. It burns fiercely and will light damp kindling.

SODIUM CHLORATE AND SUGAR

Sodium chlorate is the basis for a lot of weedkillers. Mix three units of sodium chlorate to one of sugar. It burns very fiercely and ignites even damp wood. This mixture is unstable and can go off if struck a sharp blow.

BINOCULARS AND TELESCOPES

Fortunately, the idea that you can start a fire by focusing the sun's rays with your glasses is a load of rubbish. If it were true, every summer doctors' surgeries would fill up with people complaining of scorched eyeballs.

However a camera or telescope lens will work. The downside of this method is that you'll probably have to take your expensive optical equipment apart to get to the lens.

Let the sun's rays straight through the lens and then move it back and forth until you get the smallest, sharpest and brightest pinprick of light. When you see a wisp of smoke, blow on it gently.

Every year, forest fires are started by the sun shining through discarded bottles. If you have a bottle, experiment to see if you can use it as lens.

> **white-hot, burning sulphur behind the nail hurts like hell and in tropical conditions will go septic in no time at all**

CAR HEADLAMPS

A car headlamp gathers light from the bulb and throws it forward in a focused beam. The same happens in reverse. Aim a headlamp up at the sun and the lens will focus the rays right back to where the bulb is.

This only works in strong sunlight. Take out the headlamp and remove the lens – the perspex screen it shines through. On some cars this is fastened by clips but on others it's sealed on and you'll have to prise it off or smash it. Take out the bulb, plug the hole and put the tinder on it. Aim it straight at the sun. If you have a magnifying glass, use that to focus the sun's rays still further. When the tinder catches, you'll want to tip it out before it damages the mirrored coating inside the reflector.

Some people claim that you can plug up the hole at the bottom of reflector, fill it with water and simply wait for it to boil.

ELECTRICAL FIRES

Car battery: there are two methods that employ a car battery, but in each case, bear in mind that you'll be wearing the battery down.

The first method is designed to create sparks to light your tinder. First, disconnect the battery by unbolting the high voltage cables from the positive and negative terminals.

Next, attach jump-leads to the terminals. Slowly bring the other two ends together. When they are almost touching, the electric current will jump the gap, creating a spark.

Jump-leads are obviously best for this because they are long, flexible and insulated, but almost all metal will carry a current – I've seen people make sparks using a couple of long spanners from the tool kit.

The second method uses the same principle as a light bulb: when you pass an electric current through a thin wire, it gets very hot.

You'll need jump-leads, or something similar, and much thinner wire – take it from a piece of non-essential electrics in the car, like the wire leading to a vanity light. Unravel it and take out a single strand. Keeping the ends free, deliberately scrumple up the middle section so it becomes a ball, then wrap tinder around it. When you attach the jump leads to the ends of the wire, the heat in the wire ball will light the tinder if the current is strong enough.

Another method is to mix tinder in with wire wool and soak in petrol. Attach the leads to the wire wool. It will quickly heat up and light the tinder.

Torch battery: you can coax a spark from torch batteries, although the 'Heated Wire' method is best, using a single strand or wire wool.

FLINT

Knocking two flints together will produce sparks – but only tiny ones. It's far better to knock metal against flint. If you have a knife or a machete, use the back of it, not the blade. If you have a mini-saw in your kit, that will do an even better job.

WOOD

Making fire from rubbing two sticks together is not easy, but it does work and is a method still in regular use all over the world. The advantage is that wood can be found almost everywhere and with practice the fierce heat produced by friction can create fire in almost any conditions.

The downside is that it takes a lot of practice to get it right.

THE BOW METHOD

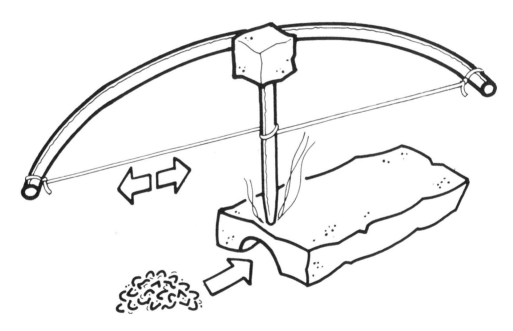

Basically you're creating a sort blunt drill, but instead of trying to make a hole, you want to make as much dust and friction as possible. Eventually the heat will light the dust and create an ember. The ember will light your kindling, and you've got a fire – but it may take anything up to two hours.

MAKING IT

There are four main elements to the bow method: a bit, a baseboard, a block and a bow.

The wood should be as dry as possible. Some say that the bit needs to be

made of hard wood and board of soft wood. Others argue that you want them made of the same wood, or they'll wear out at different rates. For simplicity's sake, use what's to hand. If you can get the right materials from the same branch, all well and good. If not, make sure the bit is harder than the board.

The bit is going to be rotating, so it needs to be straight, round, about 25 cm long and 2-3 cm thick. The bottom end needs to produce as much friction as possible, the top end as little, so carve the ends as in the diagram.

The baseboard needs to be around 30 cm by 10 cm. It's got to be long enough to steady it with your foot while you work, so if 30 cm isn't long enough, adapt.

The block needs to hold the bit steady while you work, so it has to fit into the palm of your hand and let you apply firm downward pressure. Make it out of wood, or the hardest, smoothest material you can to minimise friction. An upside-down jar can work just fine.

The bow should be 60–70 cm long. It doesn't have to be sprung, but you may have to notch the ends to take the cord.

MAKING IT WORK

Dig a slight depression in the baseboard at one end and cut a notch from the edge of the board to the depression. This where you want to glowing embers to fall. Make an ember pan out of a flat piece of wood or bark. This stays under the notch to catch the embers. You'll be putting tinder onto it to make the first flames, so bear that in mind.

Slip the bowstring over the bit and get into the position shown in the diagram. Everything should be as steady as possible. Try and steady the block against your shin and keep that foot planted firmly on the baseboard. Put your driest tinder by the notch on the ember plate.

Start drilling by moving the bow back and forth. You're balancing different elements here: the speed and angle of the bow as well as the angle of the bit and the downwards pressure on it. It's important to keep the bow horizontal and the bit vertical.

What should happen is this: friction from the bit bores dust from the baseboard and heats it to burning point. When you see smoke coming from the tip of your bit, carry on for another half minute, then put the bow and bit aside. You may have to coax the ember free of the baseboard on to the ember tray. Blow softly but firmly until you see it glow strongly, then add tinder. Blow again, and when it flames, put it into the fire.

In hot, dry climates, practised fire makers can develop enough heat by rubbing a much longer bit between their palms. After that, the principle is the same.

THE FIRE PLOUGH

Another friction method, this relies on pushing a hardwood 'plough' up and down a groove cut into softer wood. The plough creates heat, kindling and embers as part of the same process. It's advantage is that you can use the plough on a fallen tree trunk with no more preparation than cutting a straight, shallow groove in it.

What you need: a baseboard, which could be any sort of soft, dry wood, and the plough, which must be a stick of hardwood 5-8 cm long and strong enough to take firm downward pressure.

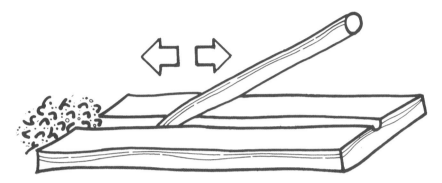

What you do: carve the hardwood into a rough chisel shape. Work it up and down the baseboard, forming a groove. It should produce long strips of wood that end up forming tinder. When the groove is about 40 cm cm long, really start to work the plough hard. The groove will darken and the dust formed by the movement will begin to smoke. Carefully add the tinder and coax into life.

KINDLING

Kindling is an intermediary stage between the tinder and the main fuel. Keep it at around a finger's thickness. Some woods burn better when stripped of their barks, and softwoods, which tend to be full of quick-burning resin, are ideal. Get used to having a pile drying out by the side of your fire.

To help the kindling to catch easily, make a few feather sticks (see above).

Among man-made materials, rubber tyres cut into finger-sized strips will take a flame in almost all conditions and burn strongly for a long time. A single strip can get a fire going in the worst conditions. They should be part of your emergency survival kit.

Plastic bottles give off a lot of heat and, like tyres, can help get things going in the wet.

MAIN FUEL

Once your fire is going, it will need a constant supply of your main fuel. I'll show you how to control the rate you burn wood below. Whether you are staying a night in one place, or a month, make a timber stack while it's still light. Make it too big rather than too small.

Use up your dry wood to get the fire going. A good hot fire will cope with wet timber – when you're experienced you can use wet wood to slow down the rate of burn.

In wet conditions you'll want to rig up a shelter to keep the worst of the rain off the wood and let it dry out a bit. Use the bottom layer for drying and the top for storage.

If you can't build a shelter, get used to dragging timber up to the fire for drying before you use it. You can prop it up near the fire, or even make a simple fire screen or windbreak out of it.

Don't waste your time and energy chopping or sawing your timber into neat lengths. Snap it into manageable lengths and drag it back to the camp. Lay long logs across the fire and let the flames get through the wood for you. For really big logs, you could rig up simple X stands either end of the fire, or wedge them between rocks.

Never try and cut wood lengthways. Split it instead. For short logs, put it on one end and make the first inroads by hammering your knife into it along the blade. Sometimes this is enough to split timber, but be very careful. The last thing you can afford is to lose your knife, either by getting it jammed into the wood or by snapping the blade by accident.

The next step is to use wedges. Make them out of hard wood, or by finding likely looking stones. Hammer them into the wood until it breaks apart.

For long branches or fallen tree trunks, hammer a line of wedges in, starting from one end and following the crack as it pulls the grain apart.

In my experience, when it's cold and miserable, you'll just burn whatever comes to hand and be grateful for it. But the more refined survivor might want to know a bit about the general characteristics of different types of wood.

Hardwoods take longer to get going than soft woods, burn more slowly and give off more heat. Soft woods burn more quickly and are more prone to spit and spark. As a general rule, the greener the wood, the more chance there is of this happening, so keep a watch out for sparks shooting out from your fire.

These characteristics can suit different uses. For example, if you have supply of both types of wood, use up the soft wood for starting a fire and when you are around to feed it. Use hard woods to keep it going when you leave the camp or bed down for the night.

When it comes to cooking, throw on softwood to get a lot of heat quickly, for a brew-up or anything that needs a rapid boil. For roasting, when you want a more steady, controllable heat, use hard woods.

OTHER FUELS

Dung and droppings from herbivores: make sure it's dry and in hot climates watch out for scorpions when you pick it up. Camels are so miserly with water that their dung is almost ready to burn without drying. Don't try and burn carnivore crap: it stinks and doesn't work.

Peat: where peat is plentiful, people have always used it as fuel. Cut it out in slabs about the size of two bricks laid side by side. Build a stack to let it dry, making sure there's plenty of space between the bricks.

Engine oil, diesel oil and hydraulic fluid: we'll take it that the engine oil you are burning is coming out of a knackered car or aeroplane, so the first job is to get it out. Almost all engines have a nut at the bottom of the casing – with old engines, you'll recognize it by the dark engine oil around it. To get the oil out, simply unscrew the nut, but have a large container ready to catch the oil.

Ideally you'll need some sort of container in which to burn the oil. Don't burn it neat. Mix it with sand to slow down the rate of combustion, or make a wick. Oil will catch light more easily when it's mixed with a bit of petrol.

To make a really hot fire, you can burn a mixture of oil and water. Pierce holes in the bottom of two cans, and make stoppers for them that can be partially removed – this is how you will control the flow of the oil and water. Hang them above a sloping trough – a bit guttering or length of split bamboo will do.

At the lower end of the trough you'll need a raised metal plate that you can light a fire under – you need the heat to get the process started. When the plate is good and hot, adjust the stoppers so that 2-3 drops of water run down the trough for every one drop of oil. When they hit the plate, light them.

Petrol: petrol is potentially lethal. It can explode and its vapour can explode, so you definitely need to control the rate of combustion. Mix it with sand in a metal container or make a lamp with a wick.

Fat and blubber: you should really be eating the fat that runs off from your animal roasts, but if there's an excess supply of fat, say from seals, make a lamp using the liquid fat and a wick. You can burn blubber directly in a stove but it flares, smokes, spits and really stinks.

TYPES OF FIRE

When you're experienced, you can adapt your fire to meet a huge variety of needs: warmth, cooking or driving insects away. Your fire can attract attention, be almost invisible, burn everything in sight, or use hardly any materials while still keeping you warm, drying your clothes and cooking your meals.

Of course, the great things about fires is that every type can do a huge variety of things for you – a simple wigwam fire will obligingly do your cooking while a cooking fire will keep you warm.

If you ring your fire with stones, you can place these round your sleeping area like night storage heaters.

FIRES FOR WARMTH

THE BASIC, BOG STANDARD WIGWAM FIRE

A successful fire depends on a number of factors: good materials, helpful conditions and a bit of skill. Make sure these are right and your chances of success are raised, but you won't get anywhere if the fire isn't set properly.

If the kindling is pressing down too hard on the tinder, the weak flames from the kindling will never get going. If it's too far away, the heat won't ignite it. The same rule applies when you're adding the fuel. Throw too much on to the kindling and you can put the fire out. Too little, and it will exhaust its own fuel.

I've always found it easier to add to fire than take away from it, so my advice is to start small and keep adding.

Make a wigwam out of your kindling so that the bottom ends of the twigs are close to the burning tinder. As the flames lick up the kindling, the sticks will catch light and, as they fall, form the hot core of the fire.

A half-wigwam can be made against a tree trunk. As the fire gets hotter, it will have something really substantial to get its teeth into.

When you add fuel, be careful at first. If possible, use easy-burning timber such as birch or other softwoods to start with, and work up from there.

LONG LOG FIRE

The long-log fire is designed to throw warmth on to you as you bivouac down for the night. With the right fuel, you can keep it going for hours. It works very well with an open-fronted shelter that keeps the draughts off your back and reflects the warmth on to you.

Gather pieces of timber as long as you like, then make a base for them with smaller sections laid at right angles to where you are going to stretch out. Lay the long pieces on top, maybe two or three deep, and parallel to your body.

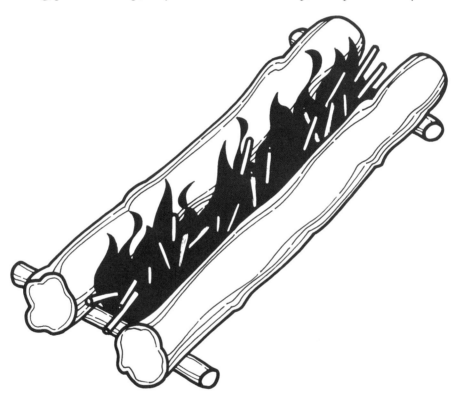

The fire will spread lengthways and keep you warm. If you are going to sleep, make sure the logs can't roll into your sleeping area.

FIRE SCREENS

You're aiming the make the greatest use of your resources. A fire in the open is only being fully used if a whole circle of people is sitting round it. Otherwise, the only radiation you're getting is what falls on your front. All the rest it wasted and your back's cold.

The answer to this is to build one or two fire screens – one behind the fire and maybe another behind your back. A fire screen doesn't have to be anything fancy: a car door will do, or four stakes hammered into the ground to support a makeshift wall of timber. But it makes the most of the heat from your fire and has the added benefit of creating an updraft which tends to suck the smoke away from you.

If you position your fire and fire screen correctly in relation to your shelter, convection currents can actually carry warmth down your back.

Don't light your fire against a rock. Use the rock as a back-reflector behind you and build a fire screen behind the fire.

If you have any metal panels, light the fire on one end and bed down on the other. The heat will be carried along it to keep you warm.

SNAKE-HOLE FIRE

These come in handy when a strong prevailing wind is making all your other efforts hard to control, and you find a suitable bank with a clear space on its lee side, out of the wind.

Hollow out a little cave in the bank, not quite an arm's length deep and couple of hand spans in diameter. Using a long, pointed stick, make a chimney by pushing in from the top. You should do this before you've finished everything off in case the stick causes a roof fall or a slab of rock in the wrong place stops you from boring down.

Make the fire under the chimney. You'll find a lot of warmth is radiated straight out at you. Because it will suck air in from the front, you'll also get a strong draught effect, meaning that the snake-hole fire can get very hot if fed a lot of wood. Alternatively, you can make it smoky and use it for preserving food.

FIRES FOR COOKING

All these fires give off a good steady heat. They're useful for all situations, but take a bit more preparation than the wigwam.

PYRAMID FIRE

This fire is strong so it can be made and left for a while, ready for lighting at a later date. Make a core of kindling, then build a tower around it, placing the layers of wood at 90 degrees to each other. Push kindling into the tower to make sure it catches. Don't go higher than about eight layers and make sure the tower narrows towards the top. The fire will catch quickly, and form a good hot core for cooking.

STAR FIRE

You'll need to get a handle on this fire when firewood is scare. It's very economical and can easily be controlled.

Get the fire going, then lay four large logs to make a cross shape, the ends meeting in the fire. To create more heat, push the ends close together; to reduce it pull them apart. If you're leaving the fire, put a flat stone over the burning ends to protect them from wet. When you get back after a couple of hours, remove the stone and blow the embers back into life, then move the ends closer in.

If the logs are of equal thickness you can balance a pot on the burning

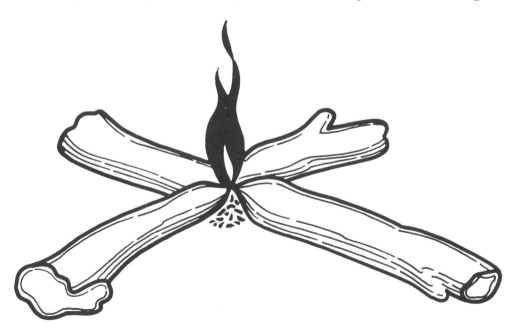

ends. If you put flat stones in the angles, you can cook food on them.

TRENCH FIRE

You'll be able to get this fire going in high winds. Dig a trench a foot deep, a foot wide and three feet long. Line the bottom with dry stones – wet ones may explode in the heat. A good concentrated heat that's great for grilling will rise from the trench.

STOVES

You've got to use what comes to hand. If you've got petrol, half fill the can with sand, saturate with petrol and use it as a cooker.

To make a wood-burning brazier, punch holes all around the base for oxygen. If the holes are small, you'll need to cut a door to stoke the fire. If they're big, stoke it by jamming a thin stick into the holes and wriggling it around.

FIRES FOR GETTING NOTICED

Being spotted from the air is harder than you think, and you've got to give your rescuers as much help as possible. That means your signal has to stand out against the background.

In the night, you'll want to build a fire that makes as much flame and as many sparks as possible. To make flames, the wood needs to be as dry as possible and the fire built up so that it lights quickly. Resinous, soft wood such as spruce and pine catches and burns the quickest.

In the day you'll want a fire that makes as much smoke as possible. Let a good, hot core develop before adding your smoke-generating material. Against a pale background, such as desert or snow, make black smoke. Anything based on petroleum by-products is suitable: oil, tar and plastic especially. Against a dark background, such as forest, make white smoke. You're in luck – leaves produce white smoke, but be careful not to smother the heat-generating core.

PRESERVING FIRE

It's so hard to start a fire without artificial aids that you'll appreciate being able to carry fire with you. African tribespeople will carry embers enclosed in slow-burning fuel, wrapped in thick, protective leaves. Those are the elements you need, although you can improvise a container from an old can and experiment with the packing.

Some oxygen will need to get through to keep the embers glowing, but too much and it will burst into flames. Feed it, check it, and keep kindling handy.

CHAPTER EIGHT

COOKING

The main reason to cook your food is to avoid getting sick. Any animal you find in the wild is likely to carry bacteria and parasites, so you'll have to cook it to make it safe. Heat kills germs. Cooking is also a handy way of disguising some of the more offputting foodstuffs. If you're eating grubs, rats and worms, you're going to need all the help you can get on the taste and texture front. Then there's digestibility: cooking starts the process of breaking down fibres and proteins in meat, and removes poisonous and unpalatable substances from some plants. I wouldn't recommend raw nettles to anyone, but young nettle shoots thrown in at the last minute are a fine addition to any stew.

Comfort can be an important factor too – don't underestimate the effect hot food can have on your morale. And cooking helps to preserve meat a while longer.

The downside of cooking is that is destroys nutrients. Vegetables in particular suffer from cooking – generally, the longer and hotter they're cooked, the more nutrients they lose. There's also the effort involved in preparing and cooking the food. In some circumstances, this can run down your energy for little reward. You'll have to weigh up the pros and cons.

BASIC EQUIPMENT

Cooking pot – ideally it's metal and you've brought it with you or found it lying round (in which case, you've washed it out well). Otherwise, you can make containers for boiling food out of green coconuts (halve them), mature bamboo (see diagram) or thick leaves that you can wrap food in for slow baking.

Pot rail – drive two strong, forked sticks into the ground and lay a third stick horizontally across the forks. Hang your pots and containers from it with short branched twigs. Also functions as a roasting spit (see below).

Pot rod – variation on the pot rail. Drive one forked stick into the ground near the fire. Angle a longer stick across the fork so one end is above the fire, and the other end is dug into the ground and weighed down with rocks. Suspend a pot from the upper end of the angled rod, cutting a notch to hold its handle, or using a pot hook (see diagram). Set up two or three rods to cook food in different containers (and at different heats).

If you don't have a pot, hang a flat stone from the end of the rod and place food on it. You'll need to experiment with raising and lowering the stone, to get the right temperature for cooking.

Pot hook – This is another way of cooking several containers at once. Cut a sturdy piece of wood, with several lateral branches, and trim the side-branches to stubs of 12-15 cm each so they point up and act as hooks for pot handles. Tie one end of the pot hook to the rail or rod. Hang your various containers on the different stubs.

Knife – or sharpened stick.

Spoon – the idea of a nice wooden spoon may appeal, but balanced against the risks of slicing a chunk off your finger, the appeal diminishes. Use a flat piece of wood instead.

Cup – useful for eating, drinking, scooping and storage, so find or make one if you can. Bamboo makes good cups – just cut out a section of the bamboo, cutting slightly below the natural join. Smooth the open end to get rid of splinters.

COOKING METHODS

BOILING

Boiling is the safest way of cooking your food. It kills bacteria and parasites and tenderizes tough meat, softens fibrous plants and keeps all the nutrients together in your pot. Never chuck water away: get used to using only what you need, and drink it when it's cool enough.

Meat: Cut meat into small pieces and boil for at least half an hour. Some nutrients will be lost in the cooking process, but the juices and fat will have gone into the water, so make sure you drink that too.

Vegetables: Vegetables lose their vitamin C when boiled, so don't overdo it. On the other hand, herbs and grasses should always be boiled to get rid of toxins and acids. If water supplies allow, boil them twice, with a change of water. Note that in high altitudes, water takes longer to boil. Above 4,000 m boiling water becomes almost impossible. For safe vegetables, always save the water and drink it later.

STEAMING

If there's bamboo around, make yourself a bamboo steamer. Cut a three-section length of bamboo, open at one end. Cut a hole in each of the two internal joins, and pour in enough water to almost fill the closed bottom section. Put your fish or veg in the top section, close it with a loose-fitting lid, and use a forked stick to prop the bamboo diagonally over the fire. When the water boils in the bottom section, steam will rise and cook the food.

If you have no way of making a container, you'll have to try the pit steaming method. Dig a small pit, heat stones on your fire till they're very hot, and place them in the pit. Cover them with leaves, place the food on top, and cover it well with another layer of leaves. Push a stick down into the food, and pack a layer of earth tightly over the top leaves and around the stick. Carefully pull out the stick to leave a small hole. Pour a small amount of water down the hole, so it hits the hot rocks and turns to steam. You should be able to measure progress by the water level vanishing down the hole, and the steam rising. Repeat if necessary.

ROASTING

Roasted meat tastes good, and is easily done by skewering meat on a pot rail and cooking over the hot embers of a fire. Initial temperatures should be very high to form a crust and seal valuable juices in the meat. Then allow the heat to die to medium and cook slowly. You'll have to keep turning the meat on the spit/rail, to avoid burning and make sure it cooks all through. If in doubt, cut some slices from the outside of the meat and eat them, while leaving the rest to cook for longer. Obviously, large pieces of meat will take longer to cook than smaller ones. For safety's sake, if you're roasting something larger than a domestic cat, cut it into several smaller pieces to cook.

In the wild, fat is something to save and use. If you roast your meat slightly to one side of the fire, you can place a tray underneath to catch the drips. Use it for basting or save for later use.

GRILLING

You can make a grill-tray out of wire mesh or by interlacing green sticks that you prop up on rocks over hot embers. Kebabing works well – threat food onto sticks and lay across the embers or flames. Grilling is fast and makes food taste good, but you'll loose almost all the fat.

FRYING

Our favourite national method of cooking is possible as long as you have enough fat (cut from a carcass or saved from earlier cooking) and a piece of metal you can give a curve to.

BAKING

This is a good method of cooking tough meat and root vegetables. It's slow, but has the advantage of not needing constant watching. You can bake food wrapped in clay or thick leaves in the embers of the fire. You'll need to parcel up the food completely so it's protected from burning. If you're using clay, let it dry around the food before placing the package to cook. You can also use a double wrap of dried grasses, with mud on top. The grasses will flavour the food. Leave the food package until the clay is baked hard. This is a convenient way of cooking fiddly beasts like fish, small birds or spiny animals, as their scales, feathers and spines will peel off with the clay. You'll still have to gut and clean animals before baking them, though.

Warning: when using leaves to wrap, be confident they're not poisonous.

HANGI

This one's for when you have no utensils or handy metal boxes, and have to rely on kindling, logs, rocks and stones. It's one of my favourites because it's so versatile – perfect for tough old meat, fish and veg. I've made a hangi last thing at night to cook my breakfast, then slept on top of it to keep warm.

Dig a pit about 40 cm deep, or five times the size of the food. Put kindling in the bottom and build a pyramid-shaped fire across the top of the pit. Start with a layer of long logs that bridge the hole, put another layer of logs at right angles to them, with a line of stones between each log. Stones should be about the size of a fist, and hard, like granite or flint. *Softer material like limestone or chalk could explode when hot.* Continue to build these alternating layers up to a total of eight or ten. Finish with stones on top. Light the kindling. When the logs burn through, the embers and the hot stones will fall into the pit. Take out the embers and ash. Wrap your food in leaves and place on the hot rocks, with meat going in the hottest middle part. Leave a gap between food and the sides of the pit. Lay young wood across the top of the pit, then heap with leaves and earth to trap heat below. The food will cook slowly – allow up to two hours or more. You can put containers of water in there to heat, too.

HEAT TRAP

If wood is in short supply but you've got a metal pot and you're lucky with the sort of litter that's lying around, make yourself a heat trap slow-cooker. Scavenge for a container of some sort, or a tough plastic bag. Pack it with insulating materials like newspaper, polystyrene or fabric. Hay or straw are even better if you can find them. Make a small fire and boil up water in your metal pot. Put your food in the boiling water, seal the pot, remove it from the fire and pack it well in to the container or bag, surrounding it with the insulation. Leave it for five or six hours to cook through. Open it and inspect. If you've got any firewood left, relight the fire and bring the pot back to the boil to kill off any lingering bacteria.

PRESERVE YOUR FOOD

This is always a good idea, even if food seems plentiful and easy to gather. Remember that circumstances change very fast and injury, illness or even the weather could stop you getting your normal supplies.

Food spoils quickly if it's warm and moist, as micro-organisms multiply in those conditions. In the short-term, food stays fresh longer if it's kept in cool places, but if it's to last more than a day or so, you'll have to change its chemical composition by drying, smoking or salting it.

DRYING

You can dry food in the sun and wind, but it will take days – maybe even weeks – and during that time, you'll have to keep it safe from scavenging animals and flies that will contaminate fruit and lay eggs in meat. Obviously, you'll also have to shield it from rain.

If you have to go for this option, cut meat into long thin strips and lay or hang it somewhere open to the wind and sun, but within arm's reach so you can get busy with swatting flies.

It's much quicker to dry food over a fire. This will result in smoking – the smoke will dry out the food and seal its surface, protecting it against bacteria. To smoke over an open fire: hang thin slices of meat over greenwood rails above a fire, so they dry slowly in the smoke. To dry fish, take out the backbone and use a stick to skewer them into position over the fire. You'll also be able to dry fruits, vegetables and plants in the same way.

SMOKE HOUSE

Build a smoke house by constructing a teepee out of wooden sticks and add cross-rails or a latticed platform to hold the food. Light a fire inside the teepee on the ground, or better still, in a pit dug into the ground. When the fire has burned down to embers, pile leaves on top (hardwood leaves are best; avoid resinous conifer and holly leaves). To keep the smoke in, cover the teepee poles with cloth or else with branches and clods of earth. Keep the fire smoking for anything up to 24 hours.

Even if the process is incomplete, you'll be able to keep meat edible for a journey.

SALTING

You can preserve vegetables by coating them in salt until you need to use them. In the wild, you can make salt by boiling seawater until it evaporates. In hot, dry climates, you will be able to evaporate a pint at a time in a shallow container.

Salt preserves meat and fish too, but must be carefully applied. In cool climates, you'll be able to preserve meat by rubbing it with salt, leaving it to hang in the fresh air, then salting again. Repeat the process for several days.

If you're in a warm climate, it's safer to boil meat and fish in a salt solution. This will have to be strong – seawater is not enough. Test for strength by adding salt to the water until a small fruit or vegetable floats in it. (Do a control test to ensure that the fruit or veg does *not* float in unsalted water.) Vegetables can also be preserved this way. Once the food is boiled, store it in the salt water until you need to eat it. You may need to sluice it in fresh water to make it palatable.

CHAPTER NINE

SHELTER

Water, warmth and food are all essential components of survival – but one that is not always given enough emphasis is rest. Without a secure, sheltered place to rest up, your chances of long-term survival are hugely reduced. Cold and wet will take a physical toll on your system, but fatigue can be equally as damaging. Survival is all about thinking clearly, and this is all but impossible when you are exhausted.

Shelters can vary from a crashed aeroplane to a quickly thrown-up wind-break or a fully-fledged log cabin. If you are lucky to have a vehicle of some sort, use it, at least at first. It will keep the worst of the elements off you.

We'll look at shelters in terms of what you may need in three different situations: when you're desperate, when you're on the move, and when you're setting up camp and looking for a semi-permanent solution.

While the main job of shelters is to keep the worst of the elements off us, they have another role: to protect us from the ground. Always try and sleep or sit on something other than bare earth or stone – leaves, heather, bracken, whatever comes to hand. This will relax your muscles, slow down heat loss and help you survive longer.

> **" shelters can vary from a crashed aeroplane to a quickly thrown up windbreak or a fully-fledged log cabin "**

Always get your shelter right during the day. To put one up at night is almost impossible, as is making running repairs if it falls down or fails to perform. Spend time on site selection. If you're in a valley, make sure you're above the flood line. You don't want to be too close to water anyway: cold gathers at the bottom of a valley, there's an increased chance of being bitten to pieces by mosquitoes, and animals might crash into you on their way to the river to drink.

The simplest shelter is better than nothing at all. If you have a tarpaulin or poncho and some para cord, you're away. Stretch the cord between two uprights – trees, saplings or sticks you have cut – and drape the covering over it. Weigh down the edges with rocks or turf, or peg them. If you can't find two uprights, just secure the cover at one end and peg the other end down. In

strong winds you may want to use this method anyway, with the low end pointing into the wind.

If the ground is soaking and you need a groundsheet, you can use an open sided tent or a windbreak, with part of the fabric on the ground. Be sure to position the open side away from the prevailing wind. In combination with a long log fire and a reflecting screen of some sort, these can keep you surprisingly warm.

DESPERATE MEASURES: SHELTERS FOR SURVIVAL

Your first priority must be to get out of the wind and rain. Cold is your enemy and the two working together on top of the effects of shock can knacker your chances of getting through the first twelve hours. Just as an indication of the windchill effect, at –1C, an 8kph wind will send the temperature to -4, and a 25kph wind will send it to –18. At –12C, an 8kph wind will send the temperature to -15,

a 25kph wind to −30. At temperatures like that, your flesh will freeze in minutes.

OPEN COUNTRY OR DESERT

The first thing to do is get out of the wind. Look for natural windbreaks – fallen trees, boulders or depressions. If you're sheltering in a depression, try and build it up on the windward side with your rucksack if you have one, or a line of stones – anything that can make a difference. If there is no shelter, sit with your back to the wind and pile up equipment behind you.

In hot desert, you'll need to get out of the sun. If you have a tent and zip-up sleeping bag, rig it up to cast a shadow. If it's big enough, fold it double and leave a gap between the layers for insulation. Leave the sides open for ventilation. Lie on something for insulation: the ground can be hot enough to cook you.

BROKEN COUNTRY

If it's light, spend some of your time looking for a shelter. If it's dark this is clearly harder. If you're on a hillside, see if you can follow the slope round until you get out of the wind. Don't try climbing up or down until you see what's around you.

Climb out of a valley bottom and try and find shelter on the slopes – but don't get yourself stuck on an exposed hillside.

A cave might be your salvation, but bear in mind that you're not the only animal in the world that needs shelter. If it's deep, proceed with extreme caution, especially if you are in bear country. Bats will not harm you, but sleeping in a shower of bat crap is not to be recommended. Look out for insects and poisonous reptiles. Don't light your fire inside a cave: build it in the cave mouth and put a heat reflector behind it.

The shelter of an overhanging rock can be enhanced by building up a windbreak in front of it.

FOREST AND WOOD

The dense needles of fallen conifers or conifer branches can provide decent temporary shelter, especially if you weave other branches through to thicken the cover. Watch out for ant-hills, though.

A fallen tree trunk can act as one wall of a shelter: scoop out a sleeping area on the stillest side and line it with leaves or cut boughs. Lean boughs over the depression, building them up until you have a decent roof. If there are dead leaves on the ground, make a layer of these and then cover with more cut boughs.

If you have a saw, select a tree with thick foliage and a relatively narrow trunk. Saw through enough of it at around shoulder height so that you can push it over without the fallen section coming away entirely. You can then shelter in the branches.

Always check the trees around you for deadfall – branches that can get dislodged in winds and fall on you. In the rainforest, you sometimes hear a tree fall of its own accord. Once heard, never forgotten – and you're very careful after that.

SNOW

Snow can be easily cut with a special saw and/or spades, but for a quick shelter, either pile it up into a windbreak, dig a trench to get out of the wind, or try and scoop out a cave in a drift. If you can make one with a narrow entrance, so much the better. Snow is a good insulator and it's possible to build the temperature up inside with your body warmth or a small fire.

If you are going to build a fire, drill a hole through the roof for a chimney, and try to create three levels: the highest for the fire, the middle for you and the lowest to trap the cold, which sinks.

A quickly built snow shelter can be a lifesaver. Imagine yourself lying curled up on the ground, and make a mound big enough to cover yourself. If there is foliage to make this, so much the better, but a pile of luggage would do. If all else fails, make it out of snow. Cover the mound with a sheet of some sort, and then heap it all over with another thick layer of snow and pack it really tight. Leave to freeze for anything up to half an hour, then make a tunnel into the mound and carefully pull out the material you have placed inside. Crawl inside and pat the roof firm. A rucksack makes a useful windbreak. If there are two of you, one of you takes the place of the padding in the middle. As the snow piles up, start to pat it to make a smooth domed roof.

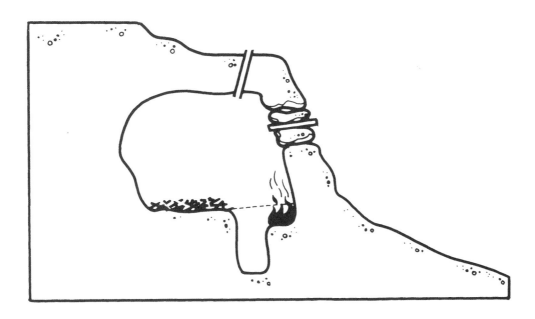

Spruce trees, the ones that look like giant Christmas trees, often have a clear space close to their trunk but completely hidden by drifts. Dig the snow out and pile it up all around up to the level of the lower branches, which you can also use for bedding. You can build a fire in a shelter like this, but make sure you set it to edge of the shelter – it will melt the snow in the branches above, and you don't want that dropping on your head.

Whenever you are in a snowy environment, always try to sit on something that will insulate you – it's possible to lose a lot of heat from too much contact. If there are trees, cut boughs to sit on and to rest your feet on.

If you have wet clothes and it is freezing outside, freeze-dry them. When you hang them out the moisture in their fibres will turn to ice crystals which can be shaken out.

TROPICAL

The leaves of many tropical trees lend themselves to shelters. Cut as many branches as you need and lay them to protect you from water. You can split the leaves of some palms down the middle and hook them over a simple frame. You should also try to get yourself off the ground, away from insects.

ON THE MOVE: SHELTERS FOR PROTECTION

These shelters vary in complexity – none is permanent, but they depend on varying degrees of skill, and this will determine how quickly you can make them. You've got to use your common sense when building them.

A-FRAME SHELTER

This is my personal favourite. The beauty of it is that it can be put up quickly but it's strong enough to stay up a long time. Not only that, but it can be customized for comfort and convenience.

The main components are the four main uprights, the roof beam, and the four rails.

Lash the four uprights to make two upside down Vs and join them across the top with the roof beam. Lash the rails at the right height for your sleeping platform. If you've got the right sort of poncho, you can thread the side rails through the poncho's sides to make your bed. Otherwise, lay smaller branches across. Tie sheeting over the roof, or use leaves, branches or other natural materials.

By making sure the side rails extend out at front and back, you can make a little table. By adding a lower rail at the side, you've got somewhere to rest your feet.

DIP SHELTER

If the shelter is built over a natural dip in the ground, bear in mind that some natural depressions are miniature bogs, while others are quite dry – it depends on the ground conditions. A small trench dug around the shelter with a run-off leading downhill will stop water running into it.

Whatever you do, make sure you're making it the right size. Lie down on the ground to get an idea of length and width, sit up to give an ideal height. Remember to include your rucksack so it doesn't have to stay outside.

If materials are limited and the shelter is going to be small, make the bed first, if possible from a layer of wood covered in foliage, and then build the shelter over it.

LEAN-TO

These are very handy where there is no shortage of wood. You can set your cross-beam between two trees with low branches or make a couple of uprights yourself. Make the roof structure with strong, light boughs or twigs, then cover with whatever materials come to hand: turf, boughs, bark – it doesn't matter. Turf makes a good roofing material, but ensure the pitch is steep enough for water to run off.

In the tropics, where bamboo is plentiful, don't lay the stems side by side, split them lengthways. Lay one split stem on its back, the next one the other way up, so that each edge fits into it's neighbour. It's waterproof, and it makes your bamboo go twice as far.

Lean-to shelters work well with long log fires and heat reflectors (see Chapter 7). Always site them with their back to the prevailing wind.

BENDER

Saplings can be tied together to form an arch or linked with a single long branch. If you're lucky enough to find them growing together, all well and good. Otherwise cut them and force them into the ground opposite in pairs. Bend the ends together and tie.

TEEPEE OR WIGWAM

Three or more long sticks are tied together at one end, others stuck into the earth to form a circle. You then cover it all with whatever material comes to hand. A parachute suspended from a branch, the skirts pinned out to form a circle, will also do the job nicely.

TARPAULIN/PLASTIC SHEETING SHELTERS

A tarp can be groundsheet and shelter rolled into one. There are any number of ways it can be used.

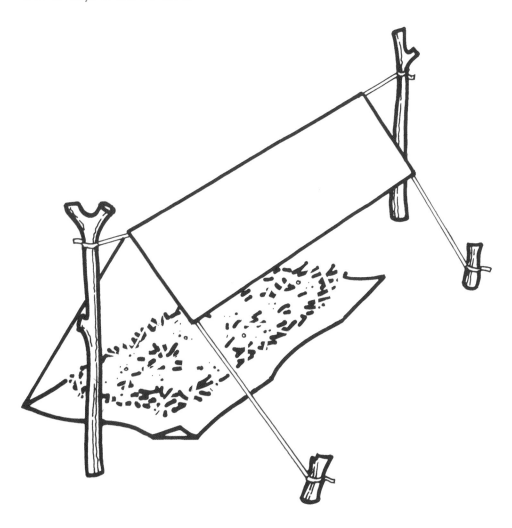

MORE PERMANENT SHELTERS

These do not necessarily take more skill to build than semi-permanent ones but will take longer and use more materials. In the case of snow shelters, including igloos, you will need specialized tools or the means by which to improvise them.

WOOD AND EARTH WALL

You can make a strong windproof wall by sandwiching earth between two outer walls of sticks. Build it up as you go. Drive in four uprights with cross-bars top and bottom. Lay the twigs that make the outer walls against the cross bars then fill the gap with earth or a mixture of stone and earth. This can form a solid barrier at the mouth of a cave or the sides of a simple, sloping roof structure.

SNOW SHELTERS

To work with snow you'll need digging or cutting tools. They save labour and stop you getting too cold handling the snow. If you want a fire, drill a narrow hole for a chimney and make sure you have adequate ventilation. Keep the fire small – a single candle will raise the temperature inside an igloo by four degrees.

SNOW CAVE

You can dig into the side of a drift, or make one inside a natural overhang, using snow blocks to form walls and narrow the entrance. Make the ceiling inside as smooth as possible to discourage drips.

Sleep on a raised platform – and dig a trench for the cold air to gather in. If you are going to block the entrance, make sure you can kick it out easily in an emergency or if it freezes in place.

TROPICAL SHELTER

In the hot, wet conditions of the tropical rainforest your priorities are going to be different. You'll want shelter above to keep off the rain, and a plat-form beneath to keep you off the floor. If you have the wherewithal to weave yourself a hammock, go for it. If not, you'll have to construct something a bit less comfortable.

The A-frame shelter is perfect for the tropics because you can stop the roof short of the ground to improve ventilation. Leaves make the best roofing material. Make a simple lattice with horizontal struts between the main uprights, and hook leaves throughout.

The atap, or wait-a-while vine, split by pulling it apart from the leaf end, can be laid or tied in a thick layer over the roof lattice. Some leaves will hang quite naturally on the lattice. Elephant grass can be woven through in no time at all. Some leaves, such as palms, have long stems that can be tied into place.

KNOTS

Survival is all about safety and cutting unnecessary risks. Imagine: you're stuck in the middle of nowhere but against all the odds have found water and food, and set up camp. Your shelter holds the rain off and you've even managed to raise the bed to keep yourself away from the insects. Then one night your bed collapses and you break your wrist.

All of a sudden you can't forage for food or firewood so easily. You get a bit weaker. Your fire goes out and you can't relight it. You get weaker still and eat a bit of meat that's gone off. Your guts play up. You get weaker still…

And it's all because you didn't know how to tie good knots.

Knowing how to make strong knots will greatly increase your chances of survival. I've arranged this section in terms of what the knots do, from tying together two ropes so they don't slip, to lashing sticks together to make a shelter.

Knots have developed for a load of different jobs – and sometimes there are alternatives. I've sorted them by job and tried to limit the options so choosing which knot to use is easier.

Don't be put off by diagrams – they can look complex. But the beauty of knots is that they have a real logic to them, and once you learn one you don't forget it.

A SIMPLE KNOT

We all know the granny knot – now's the time to forget all about it. Learn the reef knot instead: it's just as simple, better at holding and easier to undo.

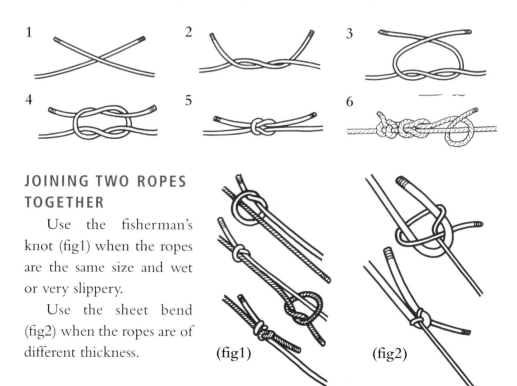

JOINING TWO ROPES TOGETHER

Use the fisherman's knot (fig1) when the ropes are the same size and wet or very slippery.

Use the sheet bend (fig2) when the ropes are of different thickness.

(fig1)　　　**(fig2)**

FOR ATTACHING ROPES TO STICKS, PEGS, BRANCHES ETC

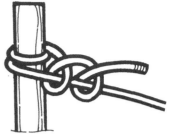

Use the round turn and two half-hitches, (see right), if something is pulling from different angles: a boat, for example or an animal.

Use the clove hitch, (see below), for hanging something from a branch that you want to untie without too much bother.

Use a round turn and two-half hitches to secure something fast.

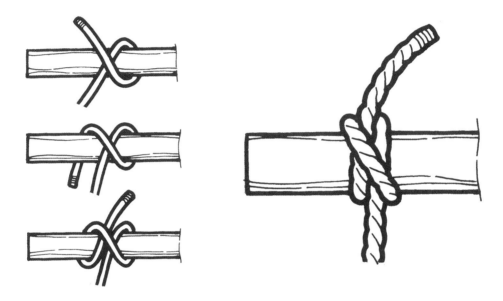

PUTTING A KNOT IN THE END OF A ROPE

Use the figure eight knot if the rope is fraying, or you want to stop it going through a loop.

FOR TYING WOOD TOGETHER

Effective diagonal lashing, (see below), is vital for building a shelter and any sort of X- shaped support. Get it right for peace of mind. Finish off with a clove hitch.

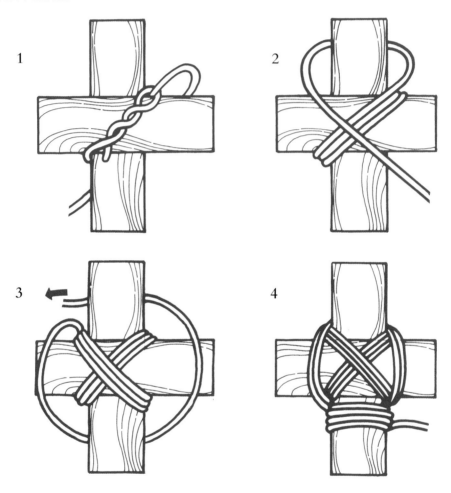

Use round lashing to extend the length of a piece of wood.

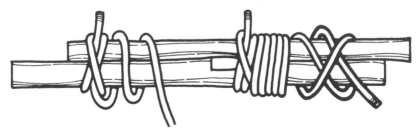

FOR MAKING HANDLES

Not hard – just follow the simple instructions. Whipping will help hold the head of an arrow as well as the blade of a knife in place.

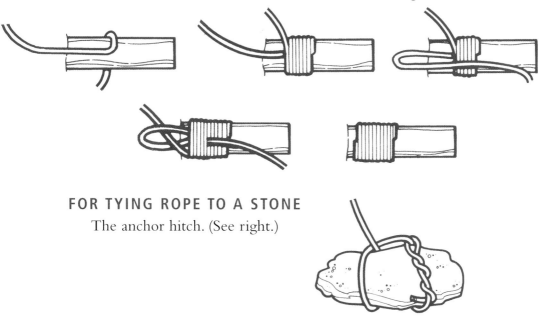

FOR TYING ROPE TO A STONE

The anchor hitch. (See right.)

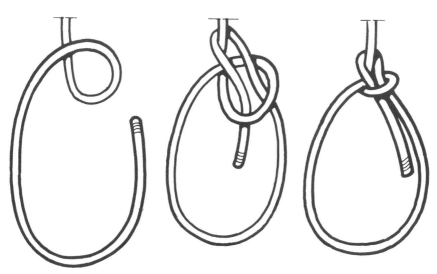

FOR MAKING A LOOP

The bowline will make a lifeline that does not slip. Use it when mountaineering.

FOR MAKING A NOOSE

Do not use the running bowline when mountaineering. If you fall, it will squeeze the breath out of you.

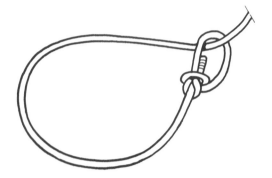

FOR MAKING A LOOP THAT WILL SLIDE ALONG A ROPE

The loop made by the prusik knot will not slip when under tension. If you have a rope fixed to a branch, you can use the knot as a moving foothold. Drape the loop over the main rope and pass it through itself twice.

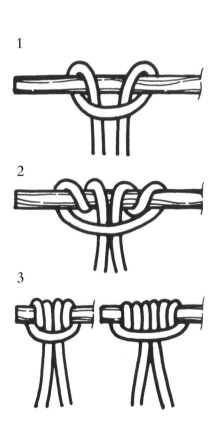

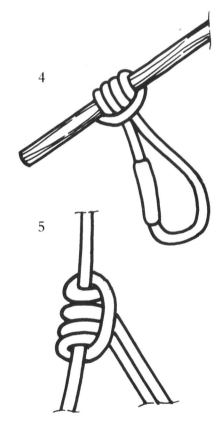

CUTTING WOOD

Anything that requires large amounts of effort should be assessed in terms of its value. For example, don't waste time cutting logs into neat lengths for a fire. Try and break them into the lengths you can drag, then just leave them on the fire to burn through.

In the Regiment we took axework and cutting so seriously that we had a rule: no cutting in the 2 hours before last light. This was in case anyone cut themselves and had to be airlifted out – leaving an hour for the chopper to arrive and an hour to get back.

Accidents did happen though – they always do with axes. On jungle training duty once an instructor was showing the new intake how to cut a path through the undergrowth with a parang – the sharp, beautifully balanced all-purpose knife the Malays carry. 'You cut like this,' he said, taking up the correct position and swiping at a tree trunk. Unfortunately the trunk was some sort of ironwood and the parang blade was unusually flexible. It bounced straight off the wood and the tip cut an inch-deep gash down his thigh. One instructor down – and I was stuck for another two weeks in the jungle. He was my replacement.

USING AN AXE

A good axe, used properly, can do anything from splitting a matchstick to building a log cabin. But to get the most out of it, you'll need to follow certain guidelines.

SAFETY

Always envisage where the axe head will follow through – should it cut through in one go or miss? All too often the first thing it will meet after the swing is a section of your leg.

Always, before using, check the head is secure.

**" Accidents did happen though –
they always do with axes. "**

PROTECTING THE HEAD

Always try to cut on to a block, never on to rock.

Don't let your axe rust up – never leave it stuck in a piece of wood.

SHARPENING

It's best to sharpen an axe with a proper whetstone, if you do not have one, use a flat rock. Angle the head at about 45 degrees and work it on the stone with a circular action. If the edge is notched, flatten it carefully by rubbing the axe-edge at a right angle to the stone. Then sharpen it. Don't put too thin an edge on an axe or it will pick up nicks.

TECHNIQUE

Don't force the swing. Let the weight of the axe do the work. If it's not making enough headway through the wood, sharpen it.

Never cut straight into the wood. Come at it from an angle – first one way, then the other. The idea is cut out a wedge, not a slit.

For delicate work such as feathering a piece of wood to make tinder, shorten the grip and hold the axe closer to the head. What you lose in power you will gain in control.

TREES

Before cutting down a tree, choose the best direction for it to fall, then ensure that it really can fall that way. A falling tree will brush though small branches easily enough, but you won't want to see it wedged in a big bough of a neighbouring tree. If necessary, clear the path of its fall – or look for another tree.

It's quite easy to make a tree fall in the direction you want. Make a straight cut no more than two thirds of the way into the bough about four feet from

the ground. This must be on the *opposite* side to the direction in which you want the tree to fall. It's not meant to bring the tree down – just weaken it so you can direct it where you want.

Make the *real cut* a good foot below this facing the direction you want the tree to fall. If using a saw, don't make a straight cut. Cut out a wedge – as if you were carving a melon.

If it's easy to climb the tree, attach a rope high up before you start. Then you can direct the fall by pulling it, after you have made the second cut and before it topples.

Do *not* start pulling before you have finished cutting – the pressure will clamp the saw blade tightly into the wood and you risk losing it.

When the tree falls, make sure everyone keeps their distance. Don't stand immediately behind the trunk – which might kick back and cause a serious injury. If standing to one side, make sure you know just how far out the branches extend.

TRIMMING

Removing the branches should be easy. If they are attached to the trunk at a slant, cut into the oblique angle.

SPLITTING

Smaller logs can be split with an axe. Anything large should be split with stones or wedges of hardwood. Work from one end, and watch for the way the grain parts. Be patient – it's a lot easier than chopping.

USING A FLEXIBLE SAW

Always keep the saw straight – jerking the handles may break it. Let the wood open naturally, away from the cut – you don't want the blade to be pinched and stuck.

If you're cutting logs on the ground, lift up one end, straddle the log and saw upwards, so the weight of the log opens the cut.

CHAPTER TEN

CAMP BASICS

If there's a chance you are going to be stuck in the middle of nowhere for more than a single night, you need to start thinking about organizing a camp.

The reason for this is simple: your camp is as important an element in your survival strategy as food and water. It's got a complicated job to do, but in essence you need it to keep you safe – and feeling safe. If you don't bother to think things through, the camp will create bad feelings and ill-health. In other words, it'll do the opposite of what you want.

LOCATION

The prevailing conditions will help you decide where to build the camp. If it's wet, materials for shelter will be a major priority. If it's blazing sunshine, you'll want shade. You want to be near a source of water but not right on top of it: the closer you are, the greater the risk of flooding, mosquito plagues and being disturbed in the middle of the night by animals coming down to drink.

In general, watch out for possible disasters.

In the desert, wadis might look tempting, but don't set up camp in them. They're not dried-up ancient riverbeds – they're more like emergency drains. If it rains heavily, you get a solid wall of water rushing though washing everything in its path away.

In mountains, watch out for rock falls and avalanches. If you're under a cliff face, make sure it's stable rock.

HYGIENE

From day one you'll have to take your hygiene level on board. In rainforest I've known camps become almost uninhabitable due to the flies and the stench because people are taking a piss too close to home.

" Watch out for possible disasters "

LATRINES

Build a latrine and make sure you use it. Latrines keep human waste in one place and encourage bacteria to start the process of breaking it down. After use, cover with a bit of earth. When or if it really starts to stink, build another.

The pit should be a bit more than a metre deep and half a metre across. If you build up the sides to make it more comfortable, make sure they are strong. You can make a cover to deter flies, and if it encourages other survivors to use it, build a shelter all around it.

WATER SUPPLY

If you have one, treat it with respect. Decide on a place to take water and make sure all washing is done downstream.

Build the latrine well away.

SOAP

Soap is formed in a chemical reaction when wood ash or seaweed ash is mixed with animal fat. If you are stuck in one place for any length of time, have a go at making it yourself.

FOOD

Within the camp, make a platform for keeping any vegetables off the ground.

Meat should be prepared well away from the camp – the blood attracts insects and predators. If you are keeping meat make wooden hooks and hang it off the ground.

DUTIES

Here's a checklist of things that should be observed every single day.

– Finding/collecting water.

– Setting and checking traps.

– Maintaining the fire and gathering wood.

– Running repairs on shelters and equipment.

– First aid.

– Working on the rescue – from maintaining the signal fire to putting markers down to guide rescue parties towards the camp.

While this book is aimed for the most part at the lone survivor, it's worth raising the subject of group duties. I've said earlier that the most unexpected people can have remarkable skills – as a group, you have to find what everyone's good at and give them a chance at exploring their potential.

Whether we're talking about self or group discipline, the point is to develop a system that ensures everything needing to be done is done – without fail. If you're on your own, make your targets reachable. If you're in a group, set priorities first and then get everyone on board.

Every group is different so there are no hard rules about anything except maximizing your chances of survival. Just remember: *discipline is not about telling people what to do; it's about creating a framework so people know what they should do, what they can do, and where the boundaries are.*

> " the most unexpected people can have the most remarkable skills, you have to find what everyone's good at and give them a chance "

CHAPTER ELEVEN

MOVING ON

Survival depends on a mix of sound decisions and basic skills. Do not move on for the sake of giving yourself something to do. The rule of thumb is that a crashed aeroplane or broken-down car will provide you with good resources for surviving – tools, equipment, shelter, fuel for fire, and, just as important – a larger visible target for rescuers.

On the other hand, if you are going to make a move, do not wait until you're so weak that your chances of making it out are nil. Making the decision is seldom straightforward and will probably involve weighing up a great many conflicting options. You will have to balance your increased need for food against the weight of carrying it or the challenge of trapping or foraging while on the move. Unless you are moving through well-watered territory, at the very least you will need something to carry water in.

Before making the decision to up sticks, run through a checklist like this, and move on only if:

- there's a good chance of finding better shelter and more food elsewhere

- you're going to starve or dehydrate where you are before rescue comes

- you think your chances of rescue will be improved

- existing dangers will be significantly reduced

- you and your party are in a fit state to move.

Ultimately it's up to you – the saying *the man on the ground is always right* applies here. Only you can balance all the unique features of your situation against each other. Whatever you do, it's up to you to *make* it the right decision.

" use your creativity and think laterally "

PREPARATION

All journeys need preparation and planning, and the more you do the better your chances of success. All the time you are in one place you should be gathering intelligence about the immediate surroundings and further afield.

If you have survived a plane or car crash, do a thorough audit of everything that could be used on the march. Even the magnet in the car's speaker system can help make a compass. Tyres make excellent kindling and sandals. Oil and petrol can be used to soak material for fire-making. Wires can be used for snares, creating sparks, and ties. Seat fabric can be torn off and sewn together for shelter and clothing or twisted for ropes. A seat frame could be adapted for a rucksack or a sledge. A compass will help you navigate; ditto any maps. Solid hub caps can be used for cooking.

Use your creativity and think laterally – but do not take equipment for the sake of it. The less you carry, the further you'll go, and whatever you do, make sure the equipment you depend on does not break down.

Take snares with you and any easily carried trapping equipment such as the wooden bits of a figure 4 trap. You may have time to set them when you camp.

If you have a source of water, work out ways of carrying some – you never know when you will need it next. Solid containers are best but plastic bags may work. A condom will hold an astonishing quantity of liquid – well over a litre. Bamboo stems can be tied top and bottom and slung over a shoulder. Carry as much as you can – anything up to five litres.

If you are climbing, prepared to get very, very cold at night as the altitude increases. Make ropes out of anything you can.

Finally, before you set out, leave a clear indication of the direction in which you are heading and your intended destination.

BACKPACKS

Make up packs – they are the best way of carrying equipment and supplies. Roll up equipment in a blanket or tarpaulin and tie off above and below the bulk at either end. If the roll is not big enough to loop over your

shoulder, make a Hudson Bay pack. Tie a knot in opposite corners of the blanket,

or fold the tip of each corner over a small stone and then tie off with a length of cord long enough to stretch from one corner, over your shoulder, across your body and back to the opposite corner. Roll your possessions up, tie the cord, and off you go.

If you're really good with knots you could try and make a rucksack frame out of branches. A word of warning, though – if it disintegrates during the journey, you're going to be left with the problem of rebuilding it or finding some other way of transporting your stuff. And this is bound to happen when you are crossing a river, negotiating a rock face or being chased

by a swarm of bees. There's a simple truth here – good equipment is built to withstand unusual stresses because those are the precise times you cannot afford to be let down.

Cut a Y-shaped bough with the upright about 30 cm and arms about one metre each. To make the arm straps, cut notches at the end of the two arms and at the end of upright. Tie rope or fabric strips from tops the arms to the end of the upright. Make sure there is enough play in the ropes or fabric to fit over your shoulders. Wrap your kit up in a groundsheet or poncho and tie it to the frame as high as possible. Pad the straps and frame with whatever you can to prevent chafing.

TEAMS

Put all thoughts of survival of the fittest out of your mind. If you are in a group and don't want morale to collapse, stick together and adopt an *all for one and one for all* attitude.

There are two main reasons for this. If the group splits into factions, no one feels safe. If one person is neglected or left behind, anyone else could be – even you. Instead of co-operating, you'll soon find you are all competing with each other and backstabbing. Stress levels are going to be high enough already without that kind of behaviour becoming the norm. Stamp on it immediately.

The second reason is practical. Everyone has different skills and different strengths. The person who lags behind on the march might be the best at coaxing a spark out of flint and steel on a cold and rainy hillside. You just don't know.

If your aim is to survive, you want to come out the other side without too much bad psychological baggage. If you stick together, not only are your chances of survival enhanced, but you'll each become a stronger person.

Teams works best when roles are defined. Everyone has something to do, and there is a shared sense of purpose. This need not be a big deal – it could be as simple as reaching a landmark for the next rest.

Choosing a leader, even on a rotating basis, is a good idea. But remember, real leadership is not about getting your own way: the true art is listening, setting targets and getting everyone to buy in to the decision.

THE BASICS OF SURVIVAL WALKING

ORIENTATION AND DIRECTION

In a worst-case scenario, you will be stranded in the middle of nowhere without a map or compass and no known landmarks in sight. If you decide you have to move on, you'll need to rely on intelligent guesswork. *Always set out with a direction or destination in mind and work out where you are at every opportunity.*

First, use the basic techniques outlined below to get a rough idea of east, west, south and north. Think of your departure and arrival places – work out from that which direction you were travelling in. Try to remember if there were any major roads or rivers connecting them, or a coastline.

In the most hostile terrain, whether forest or desert, people gather around rivers. Always follow water courses downstream always. Similarly, electricity pylons and pipelines always lead somewhere.

> " Be realistic about what you can achieve, some days can be bastards and you are not going to get as far as you want "

GETTING LOST

The most important thing is to admit that you are lost, so the group can retrace steps to get back on the right track.

PACE AND FORMATION

Adapt to the slower members of the party. The most economical walk in terms of energy conservation: slow and steady with straightish legs and swinging arms. Arrange for regular rest stops and stick to them. It could be five or ten minutes every half hour – adapt to conditions. Don't take your boots off mid-walk – your feet may swell and you'll never get them back on again.

Adopt a formation and, if possible, an order. Have one of the stronger walkers bring up the rear so that stragglers don't get left behind. In extreme conditions – cold, fog or darkness for example – tie yourselves together.

Be realistic about what you can achieve. It's good to have objectives, but some days can be bastards and you are not going to get as far as you want. Much better to set up camp when there is plenty of daylight than to struggle on and try and cope in the dark.

In general aim to average three kilometres per hour. In jungle this may drop to one per day. In bamboo thickets you may not be able to travel more than a couple of hundred metres.

SKILLS AND TECHNIQUES

Without the right skills, trying to understand a map is like trying to understand a foreign newspaper. Fortunately, learning to map-read is considerably easier, and with a compass you are well on your way to reaching a good understanding of the terrain you must cross.

But maps aren't the only way to read the landscape, and a compass isn't the only way to orientate yourself. What is more, in order reach your destination safely, there are vital skills you must know about crossing terrain.

We'll go through the technical skills first in this section – map reading, plotting a course and so on – before going on to the more practical ones: everything from finding due north by using your watch to crossing a fast-flowing river.

MAPS

To read a map properly, you must be able to turn a flat piece of paper into a landscape in your mind. There are two advantages to this. In the first place, by looking around you and noting natural features, you may be able to work out on a map where you are. This is obviously vital. In the second place, map reading will help you plan your journey, anticipate hazards and measure your progress.

Suppose you're looking at the day's journey ahead from your camp. You see hills on either side of a valley. That's the direction you're going. The valley floor bends to the right in front of you, exactly where the valley sides turn into steep precipices. The chances are you'll choose to walk along the valley floor. It's taking you in the right direction and you don't fancy starting the day with a steep climb up the sides of the valley. However, if you had been able to read a map, you might have done something very different.

CONTOUR LINES

The squiggly lines on the map show the contours of the ground, and if you have been able to read them, you would have seen that the valley floor plunges down in a series of steps at exactly the point the sides become unclimbable. If you go via that route, you'll have to stop and turn back and climb higher up – from where you are now. The contour lines are also showing that if you did make for higher ground now, you could walk more or less on a level around the side of the valley, avoiding the impassable section, and keeping above the cliffs. Once through there you're back on open ground. Now the decision has boiled down to this: waste half a day or not? Not a difficult choice.

Contour lines always record a fixed distance between two points on the ground. Imagine being in a balloon looking at two white crosses painted on a flat field. Now imagine what would happen if the crosses, still the same distance apart, were painted on the side of a steep hill. From the air they would appear closer together.

That is the key to contour lines on a map. When contour lines are their furthest distance apart the ground is flat, or only rising or falling gently. When they bunch together, the slope is steep. When they are on top of each other, the slope is vertical. The numbers written on the lines refer to the distance above sea level, and indicate whether the ground is rising or falling.

Certain natural formations translate into certain patterns on the map, and you should learn these.

Steep slope
Gentle slope
Valley
Saddle between two hills
Peak

GRID REFERENCES

Almost all maps are covered in a grid. The vertical lines show you north and south on the map, the horizontal lines east and west.

The grid also helps you pinpoint the positions of objects on the map. Along the map's edges you'll find numbers for each of the grid lines. To tell someone in which square an object or feature is, you must read off the corresponding numbers, working from left to right and bottom to top. This is called *eastings followed by northings* and is always the order in which to give a map grid reference. For example, if the object is in the square whose bottom left hand corner is where the easting line 12 and the northing line 25 meet, it's in square 12–25. That's called a four-figure map reference.

To pinpoint the object or feature, the square is divided into tenths. An object slap bang in the middle of the square would be at map reference 125–255. That's called a six-figure map reference.

This is very important for planning a day's journey and letting people know where you are heading so they can follow.

ORIENTATION WITH A COMPASS

For this it helps if you have a Sylva-type compass. These have an adjustable outer ring, a perspex base plate, and markers along the end and side. At one end a large direction-of-travel arrow is marked on the perspex base.

Make sure the compass is set so north on the dial is aligned with the direction-of-travel arrow. Put the compass on the map with its straight edge along a vertical grid line and move compass and map until the compass needle is aligned with north on the compass dial. Now your map is aligned too.

TAKING A COMPASS BEARING FROM A MAP

Provided you know where you are starting from and where you want to go to, this will help keep you on track and not go wandering off.

Divide your journey into manageable sections, each one marked by some feature on the map that you have a chance of recognizing when you get there. What you are going to do is work out in which direction you have to walk to reach the next leg before you set out. This means that if the terrain or conditions stop you seeing where you want to go – forest, for example, or cloud – you can still find the direction from your compass.

Let's call the points that mark the different sections A, B, C etc. To take a bearing of A to B, the first leg of your journey, lay the edge of the compass base between the two, with the direction-of-travel arrow pointing in the direction you are going. Holding the compass steady on the map, adjust the dial until the orientation lines are parallel with the grid lines on the map (the orientation lines are closely spaced lines within the compass dial). Read off the grid bearing and make a note of it. Hold the compass level and let the needle come round to the direction-of-travel arrow. That is the direction you walk in.

TAKING A COMPASS BEARING FROM THE LANDSCAPE

Point the direction-of-travel arrow at your destination. Swivel the dial so the orientation lines line up with the needle. Make a note of the number on the dial that lines up with the direction-of-travel arrow. When you walk, follow the direction of travel arrow, checking that the number stays in the same place.

Of course, you'll get a stiff neck from constantly checking the compass, so try and get a fix on something in the distance that's in your path, or at least attempt to keep within a fixed distance of your target.

MAGNETIC VARIATION

All I've said has to be qualified, however, because there is a fly in the ointment. There are actually two different 'Norths' – or three if you count the grid lines on the map.

Magnetic north is where the compass needle points, so it is what you will be using on the ground. Unfortunately it's always moving around due to flux in the earth's magnetic field, so is not totally accurate. Some maps carry information on the difference between magnetic and true north. To be completely accurate, add the variation to your map bearing (true north) when applying it to your compass bearing (magnetic north). Subtract the variation when you are applying your compass bearing to your map bearing.

But I wouldn't spend any time at all worrying about this while on the march. This is a classic case in which you want to be smart, not clever. The most I'd ever do is compare magnetic north to true north by aiming the compass at the pole star. If there was a significant difference I'd make tiny adjustments, but no more than that. Fiddling around with minute variations when you are cold, tired and hungry can create serious stress and disagreement in a party, or profound depression if you are on your own. My advice: use your common sense and be grateful you're moving in the right direction.

ORIENTATION WITHOUT A COMPASS

A compass is just a device for telling you where north is. It has advantages – it can help you take a bearing and it will work whatever the conditions –

but there are plenty of other ways of finding which way is north – and of course, once you know that, you know where east, west and south are too.

DIY COMPASS

A compass works on a simple principle – any piece of magnetized, ferrous metal that is allowed to swing freely will point to magnetic north. A needle is ideal.

1. To magnetize it, stroke it gently *in one direction only* on a piece of silk or against a magnet. If you think you don't have one handy, you'll find one at the base of every loudspeaker – so look in radios, walkie talkies and intercom systems. Brushing an old fashioned razor blade gently back and forwards against the palm of your hand will work as well.

2. Alternatively, float a piece of paper on a still pool of water and rest the needle on that. The needle will turn until it points north/south. When you are on the move, tie a piece of cotton around the middle of the needle or razor blade and let it swing until it stops.

Of course, this will only show you a north/south axis, so you will have to work out which is which. Watch the movement of the sun – it always rises in the east and sets in the west, so if the sunrise is on your left, you should be facing south.

Warning: all compasses can be disturbed by deposits of iron. If the rocks nearby contain a lot of iron ore, your compass will swing towards them. Similarly, move away from a car or plane to take a reading in case the vehicle is setting up a magnetic field.

PLANTS

Vegetation can give a rough indication of north and south. The South African north pole plant always leans to the north, while the leaves of the North American compass plant point north and south like old fashioned signposts.

Plants will tend to favour the sun, which means that the thickest growth will be to the south in the northern hemisphere and the north in the southern hemisphere. On a felled treestump, the rings bunch more closely together on the southern side in the northern hemisphere and vice versa south of the equator.

Moss, which loves shade, will be thicker on the northern side of trees in the northern hemisphere and on the southern side in the southern.

USING THE STARS

In the northern hemisphere, the north star will always show you true north. It's not the brightest star in the night sky and you'll have to find it by its three closest constellations – to the west of the Plough, the east of Cassiopeia and above Orion.

You can pinpoint it exactly at the intersection of two lines. One runs from the last star in the Plough's 'handle', to the bottom star in Cassiopeia. The other extends upwards from the last two stars in the Plough. The north star sits where these two lines meet.

Finding south in the southern hemisphere is a bit more complex. Locate the Southern Cross, which sits on the edge of a dark patch inside the Milky Way. Extend a line downwards through the longer of its arms. Keep going for only four and a half times its length. Stop, and drop another line straight down to the horizon for due south.

Because stars appear to wheel across the sky, you can fix a rough position by using their movement. You should use this method when broken cloud is hiding the north star or the Southern Cross.

Fix two sticks in the ground and line them up on a bright star. You are facing:

- *south* if the star is moving in a flattish curve to the right.
- *north* if the star is moving in a flattish curve to the left
- *east* if the star is rising
- *west* if the star is falling

NAVIGATION BY THE MOON

Watching when the moon rises can give you a rough east/west orientation.

- If it's up before the sun sets, the illuminated side will be in the west.
- If it's up after the sun sets, the illuminated side will be in the east.

Quarter moons can give a rough indication of north and south.

- If you are in the northern hemisphere, a line dropped from the two points of the crescent will roughly indicate south, where it hits the horizon.
- If you are in the southern hemisphere, a line dropped between the two points of the crescent will roughly indicate north, where it hits the horizon.

NAVIGATION BY THE SUN
USING YOUR WATCH

For this to work, your watch must be set to local time, so that at midday by your watch the sun is at its highest point in the sky.

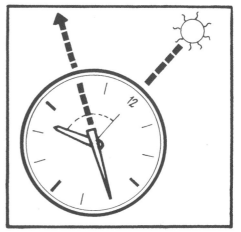

At midday only, exactly twelve noon, in the northern hemisphere the sun will be due south, while in the southern hemisphere it will be due north.

At any other time: in the northern hemisphere, hold your watch level and aim the hour hand in the direction of the sun (this is very hard near the equator where it is almost overhead). Bisect the angle between the hour hand and twelve to find a rough south. In the southern hemisphere this technique will give you rough north.

USING STICKS AND STONES

At dawn, the sun will throw a shadow roughly westwards from a long stick planted in the ground.

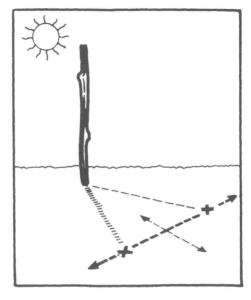

If you're not up, follow the shadow around the middle of the day. It is shortest at midday and pointing north in the northern hemisphere and south in the southern hemisphere.

At any other time of day, plant your stick and place a pebble where the end of the shadow falls. After fifteen minutes or half an hour, the shadow will have moved; put another pebble at its end point. A line drawn between these two points will lie along an east/west axis. Use this method during rest stops when you're on the move.

WALKING IN A STRAIGHT LINE

A party can keep going in a straight line across featureless terrain using an old surveyor's technique. You need at least three people to make it work.

The first person walks in the direction of travel and stops when they are still close enough to see the other members of the party, who direct them to the left or right to make sure they are precisely aligned. The second sets off, leaving the third person to stay put. They walk past the first person and on, looking back to check their alignment with the first and third people. When they have gone as far as they can, they stand still and the third person walks past the first then second people, keeping on the right track and making sure they are aligned.

It's a painstaking process but its beauty is that the person who is actually moving across the ground does not have to do so in a straight line. They can walk around obstacles provided that they end up with the other people in alignment.

USING TECHNOLOGY

The most widely used new technological gadget in navigation is the GPS, or global positioning system. A small handheld unit will pickup signals from satellites and use them to calculate your position. This is fantastic if you need to know your location to the nearest few metres – if you're negotiating your way through difficult terrain or calling for an air drop or airlift – but the machines have their drawbacks.

Firstly, like all technology, it can break down. The actual devices are strong but not infallible. What's more, the satellites from which they take their readings are controlled by the US military, which shuts them down when they need to. During the last Gulf War I remember reading about a New Zealand lobster fisherman who lost every one of his pots. He had marked their positions using GPS, but during the conflict the system was turned off to civilian users, and by the time it came back on again, every one had been carried away.

During the filming of the Arctic section of *Hunting Chris Ryan*, I experienced other problems very vividly. The devices use a lot of battery power and in the extreme cold could not get enough juice from their cells. I had to surround mine with chemical hand-warmers to raise the temperature enough to get a signal.

The second problem involved the human/machine interface, so to speak. One of the effects of hypothermia is extreme disorientation – it's like being legless but much, much more extreme. I read off the figures from the screen into my radio three times, and three times gave a different map reference. That was what the cold had done to my senses.

COPING WITH EXTREMES: different terrains and difficult conditions

Whatever the terrain or condition, dealing with them involves putting one foot in front of the other and carrying on until you reach your destination. Nevertheless, there are ways that you can minimize risk and conserve your strength, thus increasing your chances of getting to your destination unscathed.

Your watchword has to be caution. Disaster – which generally means death – can be just around the corner for even experienced survivors, as recent events reminded me. As you know, my last TV series involved my getting dropped in a challenging terrain and having to tab out while being pursued by local Special Forces. The problem was that during the Siberian part of the series, on the day I was dropped off the temperature dropped from –29C to –46C, and I didn't have the resources to survive. After four-and-a-half days I had frostbite and hypothermia. Stress, caused by the extreme cold, meant I kept on having flashbacks to the Gulf War and my long walk across the Iraqi desert.

Making things worse was a strange conviction that grew and grew in my head telling me that base camp was through a particular gap in the trees. I kept on looking at this gap and even though it was off my known route, the more I looked the more certain I became that I needed to head in that direction. Even when I saw the supply helicopter landing at another place altogether, I was still pretty much certain that my conviction was right. Fortunately, reason did prevail in the end and I was able to radio into the base camp and give them a bearing on which to look for me, plus details of a couple of distinguishing features on the landscape. If I'd followed my instincts, I would have died.

Interestingly enough, in Honduras, where I filmed another section, in spite of the extreme heat, the tiredness and incredible discomfort caused by insects my stress levels were much, much lower. It reminded me that cold can kill you in lots of different ways.

NIGHT TRAVEL

In hot desert conditions, travel by night and rest up by day. There are a number of reasons for this:

- by lying up during the day, you can conserve moisture
- it can get really cold during the night – you'll be grateful to be cracking on
- clear skies make for easy navigation by stars.

If you have to move over more broken terrain by night, always wait until you have proper night vision. This will take at least thirty minutes to develop and can be ruined by even lighting a match. If you are relying on a map, try and rig up a red filter for your torch.

> **if conditions are bad or you're walking in extreme darkness, rope yourselves together**

You'll find that the corners of your eyes are more sensitive to light and movement than the middle. If you're trying to make something out, look at it out of the corners of your eyes. Conversely, if you see something out of the corner of your eyes, don't dismiss it if you can't see when looking straight at it. Your eyes may be playing tricks, but not in the way you think.

If conditions are bad or you're walking in extreme darkness, rope yourselves together.

Don't try crossing broken terrain in darkness, unless you are really desperate.

Break camp and get packed up before it gets dark, or you're bound to leave something behind.

ARCTIC

In arctic conditions, the cold attacks your body and your mind. Any exposed skin is liable to get frostbitten, and long before that happens your hands will be numb to the point of being useless lumps (see chapter on first aid).

Extreme cold gives rise to stress, and stress both tires the body and confuses the mind. It also makes you produce more urine, making dehydration a threat. If you haven't been able to make fire, don't drink icy water, which will cool you down even more. You should try and melt about a litre per day, as outlined in the chapter on water.

The effects of hypothermia, or exposure, are rather like being unpleasantly drunk. You can't walk or think straight at the very time you need to be in full charge of your faculties. If you're on your own, you must get out of the wind and if possible, get into dry clothing, a sleeping bag or a survival blanket. Even a plastic groundsheet will protect you from the wind. If you're with others, check by asking each other simple questions. If someone gets it wrong, they're probably in the early stages of exposure.

Always get out of the wind when you can. At −14C, a 30kph wind will drop the temperature to −30C. A 60kph wind will drop it to around −40C.

DRESS

Multiple thin layers that insulate by trapping warm air between them is the ideal get-up. The new synthetics are best but wool takes a lot of beating. Mallory almost climbed Everest wearing layers of wool, flannel and a tweed jacket.

Outer layer: should be windproof and waterproof. Make sure you have covering over your face, including your cheeks, to prevent frostbite. Fur trim keeps the wind off your skin.

Inners layers: if you lack new, insulating synthetics, go for cotton and wool. Wool is slow to absorb water and so maintains its properties best of all. If you find yourself sweating, either stop the activity or remove clothing – damp causes clothing to lose its insulating properties.

Hands: mittens are better than gloves. Use spare socks if nothing else is available. In extreme cold, your hands can lose their ability to function in seconds.

Feet: thick boots with thick soles to insulate your feet. 1-2 cm for the boot and three layers of sock is perfect.

Eyes: If you don't have proper goggles you'll need to improvise against snow blindness. Camera film, cardboard or bark with slits cut into it will work for a while and be better than nothing. Cut a nose-piece and tie it round the back of your head.

TRAVELLING ON SNOW

We tend to think of snow as soft, white stuff and find it vaguely amusing that Inuit people have so many different words for it. But when you've come up against snow that's so cold it's like sand or so fine that it's like flour, or so dense that it's like ice, you begin to understand them.

Walking through soft snow in normal footgear is exhausting. Snowshoes spread your weight over a larger area and stop your feet plunging into the snow. Skis, whether manufactured or improvised, have the added benefit of allowing you to glide but are not suitable for broken terrain.

Cut yourself a stick about shoulder height. You can use it to test ice for strength or knock snow off branches. If you fall in the ice, jam it across the hole and haul yourself out with it.

NAVIGATION

If you're near the coast or on the ice pack, don't take a bearing from an iceberg. It's probably moving.

SNOW BLINDNESS

When you stare at sun on snow for any length of time, you go blind. If you do not have dark glasses, cut slits in some bark, cardboard or fabric, and use it to cover your eyes.

WATER

Don't get wet if you can possibly help it. If you have to cross ice-cold water, remember that if you are immersed your body loses one degree centigrade every two minutes. You have around eight minutes before you fall unconscious, and about a quarter of an hour before you die.

If you are wading in a river, strip off and put your clothing into a bin bag to make sure you have something dry to put on when you get to the other side. If you have proper waterproofs, wear them or use them as flotation devices (see section on river crossing further on in this chapter). On the other side, try to light a fire to get your body temperature up.

HOT DESERT

I specify *hot* desert because in some areas of the Middle East during the winter months you are more at risk from hypothermia than dehydration. In the Iraqi desert in February, I walked at night simply to keep warm and lay up during the day when the temperature rose a little.

In hot desert, however, your main enemy is dehydration – so make finding water your main focus of activity. To put things in perspective, in temperatures of around 50C, you will last no more than two-and-a-half days without water – *if* you have found shade and *if* you do nothing at all.

If you start to walk in the heat of the day, you will get no further than eight kilometres before going down. Bear this in mind before you set out on a journey.

With a litre of water and walking at night, you might get as far as 80 km and last up to two-and-a-half days. Walk steadily, trying to breathe through your nose only. This will reduce the amount of water you exhale and stop your mouth and throat from drying out.

Camels can absorb a vast amount of water at one go, and then ration it out over a long period of time. You can't. Your body will absorb what it needs and then excrete the rest – effectively wasting it. So take water in small sips rather than in big, infrequent binges. A good way of rationing water is to work out how long you will last with available supplies and divide the one into the other. Give yourself a little bit every hour, or, if supplies are very short, at greater intervals.

DRESS

Cover as much of your body as possible with a layer or two of thin fabric. This slows dehydration and will reduce sunburn.

> **in temperatures of around 50C, you will last no more than two-and-a-half days without water - if you have found shade and if you do nothing at all**

Wrap rags around the tops of your boots or shoes to prevent sand getting in, which chafes the skin and causes blistering or sores.

NAVIGATION

If you are travelling by night, use the stars. By day, use any one of the methods described above to take a rough bearing from the sun.

SAND BLINDNESS

Like snow blindness, its primary cause is glare, but in the desert this is made worse by grit and blown sand particles. Make goggles by cutting slits in cardboard or fabric.

WADIS

These are steep banked, dry river channels cut into the desert by water. Although they're dry most of the time, they flood quickly and dramatically during desert storms and practically everything in them is carried away.

MOUNTAIN AND ROCK FACE

Mountain slopes are inhospitable places and normally the rule is to get down, if possible, to a milder microclimate in a valley or on the lower slopes.

Never underestimate the danger of trying to negotiate mountains in fog or darkness. Even well-known, some would say crowded mountains like Snowdon claim lives regularly, often as a result of walkers getting lost in poor light or fog. When visibility falls, so might you. If you are caught outside in an electrical storm, make sure you are not the tallest thing around. Lie flat or stoop. Do not shelter under a tree that might attract the lightning.

Unless you can make your way down in relative safety, you probably have a better chance of long-term survival by staying close to a crashed aircraft and making every effort to dig in and attract rescuers.

When climbing or descending a rock face, always maintain contact with the rock in three places – two hands and a foot, or two feet and one hand. This will give you stability. Climbing is very tiring unless you are used to it, so don't embark on a climb unless you are confident you can get to the top before your limbs give out.

ROPE WORK

Using a rope on your own is tricky, but there may come a time when it's the only way. Obviously, if you can tie the two ends together at the top, when you get to the bottom you can untie them and free your rope. But if that reduces the rope's length too much and you find yourself having to secure one end, make sure you're actually getting somewhere by sacrificing it.

Although they look horrendously precarious, I have used snow bollards and I know that they work. In hard snow, cut a snow bollard at least 30 cm deep and 1m wide. In soft snow make it three metres across. In ice make it at least 15 cm deep and 50 cm in diameter.

Pad the rope with anything available to stop it cutting through the bollard, and go.

STEEP SLOPES

Climbing or descending, make sure you zigzag. In snow, the leader should try and beat a level path for the rest of the party, but make sure everyone fit takes a turn. As a rule, walk on your heels to stop yourself sliding or tipping forwards.

If you begin to slip sideways on a scree, go with it. Keep turned sideways to slope, as upright as possible, and try and move across to the other side.

AVALANCHE

There is not much you can do with an avalanche. Don't try to outrun it – try and get to the side. If you feel you are crossing a potential avalanche slope, keep quiet, move slowly and proceed one by one.

If an avalanche does catch you, try and 'swim' it with your arms and legs. The longer you stay on top, the less deeply you will end up buried. If you become trapped, try and clear a breathing hole by moving your head forwards and back and from side to side. Let yourself dribble to see which way is up and which is down. Try to get out as quickly as possible.

RIVERS

Rivers can be seen as barriers or opportunities. In parts of the world where the conditions make travel hard – whether dense forest or marshy tundra – rivers are the motorways and you've more chance of finding a potential rescuer there than in the middle of nowhere.

However, there will be times when you have to cross a river – and that's when you'll find out why, since time immemorial, they have defined national boundaries, and held up armies.

It's often hard to follow a river by land. If the ground is level, the chances are you'll have to make wide detours round marsh or water meadow.   If the ground is hillier, the river might well have cut itself narrow gorges that you cannot negotiate. Best to try and find a level contour some way above the river, and follow that.

RIVER SENSE

Prepare to get wet. That means putting all fire lighting equipment and a change of clothing somewhere dry in your luggage. Wrap them up in layers of plastic, if possible, and put them in the middle of the pack. Use waterproofs, which shake dry, as protection, or as flotation devices made by tying off the waist and legs so that air can be trapped inside.

If you're going to cross, remember that a river will only get deeper, wider or faster as it travels to the sea. If it's uncrossable where you meet it, try it further upstream.

Always take into account the effect of the current and set off upstream of where you need to land, so you are crossing the current at an angle.

Whether you are crossing or planning to float down, study the river as much as you can. It will still surprise you, but at least you will have anticipated some of the shocks. Waves that bulge at the same place on the surface of the water indicate a rock on the bottom. You'll often find dangerous eddies where rocks almost break the surface of a fast-running river. The swirling water here can pull you back and down.

Watch out for waterfalls – no one's got a survival plan for them.

CROSSING

Every year you hear of tragic drownings in flooding rivers. It's my belief that a lot of these are due to over-familiarity – people know the river when it's quiet but cannot believe the power of the water when it's in flood. Never underestimate the power of water – and if you do get swept off your feet, try not to fight it. The chances are that you will lose.

WADING ON YOUR OWN

If you're on your own, cut a long, strong stick. It will stabilize you like the third leg of a stool and act as a break against the force of the water. Dig it in downstream and lean against it if you need to.

Take off your trousers to reduce resistance to the water – you don't want the water to tug you. Remove socks to keep them dry but put your boots back on. You must wear some foot protection to cross.

Face slightly upstream, so you can keep an eye out for objects being swept towards you. Shuffle, rather than stride, across, using the stick to balance you and probe for dips in the riverbed.

Loosen your pack so you can get it off quickly if you fall. Don't let go of it, though – it will probably float and may protect you against rocks.

WADING IN A GROUP

Divide into groups of three of four, each forming a tight circle, holding each other's shoulders. This makes the group strong and stable and allows them to watch out in all directions.

A long stick or light tree trunk held firmly at about chest level can give a group stability.

If there is only one support stick, give it to strongest member and have the others hold on to him or her.

If practical, make a line downstream of the strongest member, so he or she breaks the force of the current.

If there are more than one competent river crossers, place them at either end of the line or interspersed through it to 'hammock' the weaker members.

ROPE CROSSING WITH THREE OR MORE

The best way is with a rope about three times longer than the river is wide. The idea is that there will always be two people on dry land anchoring the one that is crossing.

Tie the rope in a loop and secure it round the chest of the first person to cross. Two others hold the rope, one at the point the first crossing takes place, the second a few metres downstream. If the person crossing falls, there will be two anchors on the shore to prevent them getting swept away. When the first crosser makes it to the shore, they untie and the second crosser ties on. They cross, with the others passing the rope between them. When the second has crossed they untie themselves while the third ties on. The first goes a few metres downstream. The third crosses, assisted by the second while the first acts as an added anchor.

SWIMMING

For all but the narrowest, calmest rivers, always try and give yourself buoyancy.

Unlike a flat, calm sea, a river is a very large volume of water in a state of irresistible movement. It really is the proverbial unstoppable force. In even the most placid-looking rivers the shape of the bank and irregularities on the bottom can combine to create dangerous eddies and whirlpools. Even if these don't suck you down, they can confuse, tire or batter you.

You must take into account that your buoyancy aid will probably slow you down. Start higher upstream than you would normally do. It's easier to float down to your landing spot than to swim up to it.

Try and let the river do as much work for you as possible. If it is flowing from left to right in front of you, cross just where it curves round to the right – the current will carry you to the other side. I found this out the hard way in Honduras where I was filmed trying to cross a river that went from left to right in front of me but then curved round in a bend to the left. There's a lot of rather frantic splashing as I try to get across the current to prevent myself being carried to shore on the same side of the river.

Strip down to swim or just wear waterproofs. Normal clothes will not keep you warm in the water. Your rucksack will make a good float. If you have lined yours with a bin bag, make sure it is tied shut with knots you can undo when they're wet. Plastic bottles will aid buoyancy but only if you've emptied them. Give yourself a drink, screw the tops back on and set off, but don't forget to fill them when you get to the other side.

Swim with the rucksack in front of you, pushing it through the water. One rucksack will support a couple of people. A few tied together can form a buoyant raft for the group. Do not try to sit on it – it will sink.

 If you do not have a rucksack but do have waterproof outer clothing, see if you can make a float by filling it with foliage and tying off the apertures. A tarp filled with foliage will also float. Don't overfill it – better you have enough free material to tie it tight.

If the water is ice cold, bear in mind that after about nine minutes, immersion you will pass out and then freeze to death. The cold may also paralyse you temporarily when you get in.

If you have miscalculated and get swept away by the current in turbulent water, try and adopt a sitting position with your legs pointing downstream to absorb the shock of hitting obstacles or to push yourself away from them.

RAFTS

You can make an armchair raft by lashing together two buoyant logs about 50-70 cm apart. When you sit in the middle, your arse will keep them apart and they will support you.

If you have a huge tarp or a large area of waterproof plastic, you might be

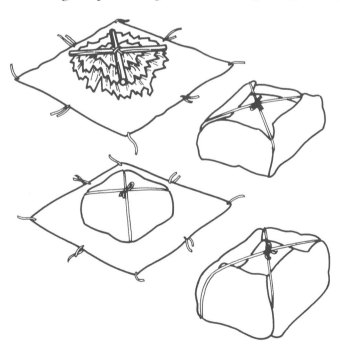

able to improvise a raft with sufficient buoyancy to hold yourself and a companion clear of the water. Lay it flat and pile up stuff that floats in the middle: brushwood, hay, anything really. Tie it tightly shut and launch it with the tied side facing up. Improvise oars from long pieces of wood with shorter pieces lashed at the end.

JUNGLE AND FOREST

In wet, hot forest, discomfort levels soar. Insect bites, parasites, sweat rashes and chafing can make life a misery while the frequent downpours make you want to scurry for shelter. But the important thing to remember is that these factors are not fatal on their own and overcoming them is a psychological, not a physical battle.

Factors to watch out for in the rainforest are infection and natural dangers from poisonous insects, snakes and predators. Even though it is humid, dehydration is a real threat in the intense heat and this will only get worse if you are having to hack your way through thick undergrowth.

DRESS

Cover up with loose clothes. Secure wrists and ankles with ties to stop insects from getting under your clothing. Lycra shorts will help prevent chafing.

Keep a dry set and a wet set of clothing. Wear the wet set during the day and the dry set at night. Keep discipline on this – although there will be nothing more horrible than putting on stinking wet clothes every morning, you will not regret it. Dry clothing will give your skin a chance to fight off any fungal infections and you will sleep better in it.

STORE WATER

Get into a routine of replenishing water supplies whenever the opportunity lends itself. Because the climate is so humid, you may not feel so dry in the throat – but this does not mean you don't need to take in fluids. Refer to the chapter on water for an indication of how much you need.

SKIN INFECTIONS

Try and treat these as quickly as you can. Microbes and bacteria flourish in the warm, wet conditions, and wounds will go septic and even gangrenous more quickly here than elsewhere.

Wash whenever you can – I recommend getting into rivers fully clothed to get as much sweat and mud off your garments.

INSECTS AND PARASITES

Insects are attracted by sweat, and there is not much to be done about it.

If you don't have chemical repellent, try smearing yourself with oil, mud, ash, even grease. Try and rig up protection for your face – a line of strips hanging loose, like the corks dangling from the hat of the mythical Aussie bushwhacker. This will help during the day; and at night, if possible, sleep under a mosquito net. However, these may only provide partial protection. The last time I was in Honduras, the mozzies were biting me through my hammock.

I've seen indigenous people light smoky fires under their sleeping platforms to keep the insects away.

Remove ticks and leeches carefully – if you pull them straight off, the head may stay embedded in your skin and fester. Leeches will drop off of their own accord when they are full of blood, but if you are covered, you will not want to wait that long. Dab them with salt, alcohol, a lighted cigarette, or anything burning hot.

Ticks drop when burned or covered with Vaseline – this suffocates them.

If you disturb hornets, run; you can die if a swarm catches you. Watch out too for large, stinging ants. They are not programmed to get out of your way so get out of theirs. Ant bites hurt like hell, but aren't that dangerous unless you get covered with them.

Bot flies, found in Central and South America, have maggots that can get under your skin. The flies are big – about the size of bees – and lay their eggs on the legs and bellies of other insects, such as mosquitoes. When the mosquito lands on you, the eggs drop off, burrow down into your flesh and start to eat you. The first you know of it is that the site begins to itch, then, as the maggots grow, a maggot-filled boil forms on the skin. If the maggots find their way into the eye they must be removed by surgery. Anywhere else on the body, you can either try to suffocate them by smearing their breathing holes (which poke out of the skin) with Vaseline or anything that will stick and block them. If this doesn't work, it won't kill you to wait for them to mature, at which point they will eat their way out and drop off.

CHAPTER TWELVE

DANGEROUS ANIMALS

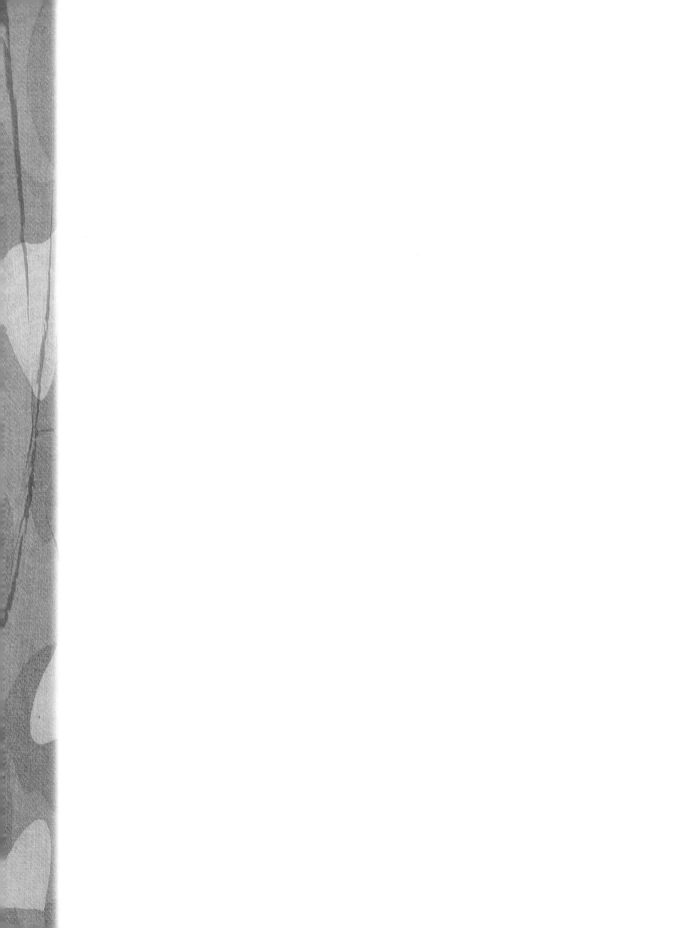

Danger comes in all shapes and sizes – and not always from the most expected source. In Africa, more people are killed by hippopotamus that any other wild animal, and the biggest natural killer in the world is the malaria-spreading mosquito.

My motto is: if it slithers or scuttles, avoid it. In Honduras during the making of *Hunting Chris Ryan*, I was relaxing in base camp with the film crew after surviving the worst the tropics could throw at me. It was night-time, and after a few drinks nature called so I crossed the camp to go to the bathroom. Just as I was about to put my foot down, something made me shine the torch on the floor. Right in front of me, exactly where I was about to put my foot, was a good-sized fer-de-lance snake. I called the crew over – which was a big mistake, because instead of moving away, the snake got into a strop. The guide saw this and made us all move back, so we retreated about ten feet while the guide took it on with a stick.

Just then, the snake attacked. It moved fifteen feet in what seemed like the blink of an eye. I turned, knocking my head into the cameraman's, who went down. Fortunately the guide had everything under control and took the snake out, but the cameraman said that all he could think of as the ground rushed up to meet him was: there's a snake down there and I'm going to join it.

This is not meant to alarm anyone – if the snake had been left alone, I'm sure it would have opted for a quiet life and made its way off. Surviving dangerous creatures is mostly about being able to understand the threat so you can react to it appropriately.

LAND MAMMALS

You're in danger from land mammals for three main reasons:

- they want to eat you
- they're protecting their kill or their young
- you're in their territory and they think you're a threat.

In the animal kingdom, killing is just a means to an end. Killing for pleasure is primarily a human characteristic.

If you're faced by a predator, there's no denying that you're in a fix. The first thing to remember is: don't run. It can probably move faster than you – bears run as fast as dogs – and may well be able to climb better.

Avoid eye contact, but face it at all times. Try to get something behind your back – a tree or a rock – and something in front of you: a pack, for example. If it does attack, curl yourself into a ball and try to wrap an arm round the back of your neck. The animal might get bored if you play dead.

If you are going to try and hurt it, really go for it. Half measures won't work. If you have fire or something burning, go for the eyes to blind it. Remember, for a predator to survive, it has to be fit. It will not want to risk an injury.

Be respectful about territory. A pack of dogs lying under a tree will think it's their tree, so give them a wide berth. Any animal eating will want to be left alone, as will nursing mothers.

Remember: your most important weapon against dangerous animals is knowledge. Before venturing into the wilds, do your research, and when you arrive, talk to local people.

INSECTS AND SPIDERS

Scorpions
territory: almost all hot climates
markings: range from yellow to dark brown
size: 2.5 cm to 20 cm
danger: extremely painful sting, but rarely fatal except in the young and old. Symptoms range from acute pain to paralysis. They like shade, so shake out piles of clothes, especially footwear, in hot, dry conditions.

Fiddleback spider
territory: North America
markings: brown with violin shape on back of head
danger: extreme tissue damage round wound; vomiting; fever symptoms.

Black widow spider
territory: hot climates

markings: hourglass on abdomen
danger: pain, weakness, sweating for a week. Rarely fatal.

Funnel-web spider
territory: hot climates
markings: brown and furry
danger: fatal. Pain, weakness, sweating.

Tarantula spider
territory: mostly equatorial Americas
markings: furry body, thick brown legs
danger: not fatal but nasty and frightening.

Centipedes and millipedes
The bigger they are, the worse they are. Watch out for clawed feet and nasty bites.

Hornets, wasps and bees
Generally speaking, the bigger the beast, the worse the sting. Watch out for nests. If you are allergic, one sting can be fatal. If you are not, being caught by a swarm could kill you. Try and cover yourself to stop more getting to you. Dive into water or get downwind of a smoky fire.

SNAKES

For the most part, snakes are as anxious to avoid you as you are to avoid them. They will only attack if they feel under threat, so be careful not to disturb them. As cold-blooded creatures, they are likely to look for warm places in cold climates and cool places in hot climates. Lever up stones and fallen tree trunks with long poles rather than your hands. Let the snake escape and then proceed as normal.

If looking for grubs around fallen tree trunks, be especially aware. Ditto, always look down if you are about to step into shade.

Some snakes will spit venom. This is not an effective way of delivering poison but you must wash it out of open cuts or your eyes immediately, with any liquid that comes to hand – even urine.

Kill a snake by whacking it with a long, heavy stick. Try and break its back as close to the head as possible.

THE AMERICAS

Rattlesnakes

territory: North America

size: 45 cm–2 m

markings: some have diamond patterned backs; they may sound the rattle at the end of their tail when alarmed

danger: the rattle is a warning. The bite can result in paralysis as it attacks the nervous system; extreme tissue damage.

Copperhead

territory: eastern USA

size: 60-90 cm

markings: orange brown, brown bands, coppery head

danger: quite timid and not usually fatal.

Cottonmouth/water moccasin

territory: water in southern USA

size: 60-130 cm

markings: dark brown/olive, blotched paler markings. Paler belly.

danger: fierce and deadly. Gangrene often occurs around the bite, needing prompt attention.

Tropical rattlesnake

territory: northern South America, Mexico

size: 1.5-2 m

markings: diamonds on back

danger: fierce and deadly.

Fer-de-lance

territory: northern South America, Mexico

size: 1.3-2 m

markings: brown with lighter brown markings

danger: fierce and deadly. Along with extreme tissue damage around the bite, massive internal bleeding will occur as the poison attacks the blood.

Bushmaster

territory: Central and South America; lives in burrows

size: 2-2.6 m

markings: pink brown, dark diamonds running down back

danger: fierce and deadly.

Coral snake

territory: Africa and South East Asia

size: 45-90 cm

markings: colourful wide black and red bands with narrow yellow ones

danger: shy but deadly member of Cobra family. Respiratory paralysis follows the bite, resulting in suffocation.

EUROPE

Adders

territory: north Europe through to Mediterranean

size: 30-75 cm

markings: zigzag down back

danger: rarely fatal in north, more dangerous the further south.

> " **your most important weapon against dangerous animals is knowledge, do your research** "

AFRICA AND ASIA

Puff adder

territory: Africa and Arabian peninsular

size: 90–130 cm

markings: straw brown, darker markings.

Saw-scaled viper

territory: North Africa to India

size: 40–55 cm

markings: pale red to sandy brown

danger: widespread, fierce, deadly.

Malay pit viper or moccasin

territory: South East Asia, Indonesia

size: 60–80 cm

markings: colour varies from fawn to reddish to grey with geometric patterns. Belly is yellow to muddy green.

danger: common, fierce and deadly. The poison attacks blood cells.

Russell's viper

territory: forest from Pakistan to Taiwan

size: 1–1.24 m

markings: light brown, ringed spots on back and sides

danger: aggressive and common. The bite is a powerful coagulant, affecting the blood and resulting in massive local tissue damage.

Cobras

territory: Eastern Africa, India, Indonesia

size: 1.5–2 m

markings: spread hood when alarmed or angry

danger: fierce and common. Respiratory paralysis leads to suffocation. Tissue damage can occur.

Mambas

territory: sub-Saharan Africa

size: 1.5-2 m

markings: tree mambas green; ground mambas black

danger: extreme. Fast and fierce.

Krait

territory: India to Indonesia

size: 90-150 cm

markings: black and white or yellow bands

danger: shy but deadly. The venom is a neurotoxin that leads to respiratory failure and suffocation.

AUSTRALASIA

Death Adder

territory: sandy parts of Australia, Papua New Guinea

size: 45-60 cm

markings: well camouflaged brown to reddish grey

danger: fatal. The venom is a neurotoxin that leads to respiratory failure and suffocation.

Australian Black Snake

territory: near fresh water in Australia

size: 1.5-2 m

markings: dark blue-black with red belly

danger: slight.

Australian Brown Snake

territory: Australia, Papua New Guinea

size: 1.5-2 m

markings: brown with pale belly

danger: fierce and fatal.

Tiger Snake
territory: Australia
size: 1.3–1.6 m
markings: tawny with darker bands
danger: common, fierce and fatal. The venom attacks the nervous system leading to respiratory failure.

Taipan
territory: North Australia
size: up to 3.5 m
markings: light to dark brown, yellow-brown belly
danger: common, fierce and fatal. The venom is a neurotoxin that leads to respiratory failure and suffocation.

RIVERS
When swimming, try to wear foot protection.

Electric Eels
territory: South America – Amazon and Orinoco
size: up to 2 m
markings: dark green to black
danger: 500 volt shock which can knock a man out.

Piranhas
territory: South America. Amazon, Orinoco and Paraguayan rivers
size: up to 50 cm
markings: greeny grey with red belly
danger: fierce bite; shoals can kill swimming mammals.

CHAPTER
THIRTEEN

SURVIVAL
MEDICINE

What is survival medicine? In a nutshell, it's what you get when standard medical care and facilities are unavailable and you're treated by people with no formal medical training. The basic assumption is that trained doctors and hospital care will be unavailable for a prolonged period of time and that in addition to providing first aid, longer term care will need to be provided.

Foremost among the many problems that may affect your chances of survival are medical problems resulting from extreme climates, ground combat or evasion, and illnesses from poor hygiene.

Almost all survivors find it hard to treat injuries and illness due to the lack of training and medical supplies but remember this: basic medical knowledge can make a huge difference to your own and other people's survival prospects.

WHAT DO YOU NEED TO KNOW?

Maintaining good health
Personal hygiene
Sterilization
Limited trauma and life-saving tips
Bone and joint injury
Insects
Snakebites and scorpion bites
Skin diseases and ailments
Gastrointestinal illness
Burns
Environmental injuries

WATER

We've dealt with this earlier in the book but to repeat: it's easy to get dehydrated even when you have a ready supply of water, so keep fluid intake levels up if possible.

You can use the pulse and breathing rate to estimate fluid loss.
• With a 0.75 litre loss the wrist pulse rate will be under 100 beats per minute, and the breathing rate 12 to 20 breaths per minute.
• With a 0.75 to 1.5 litre loss the pulse rate will be 100 to 120 beats per

minute and 20 to 30 breaths per minute.

- With a 1.5 to 2 litre loss the pulse rate will be 120 to 140 beats per minute and there'll be 30 to 40 breaths per minute. Vital signs above these rates require more advanced care.

The following is an easy formula for making an oral rehydration fluid.

- $^1/_4$ tsp salt (sodium chloride)
- $^1/_4$ tsp lite salt (potassium chloride)
- $^1/_4$ tsp baking soda
- 2 $^1/_2$ tbsp sugar

Combine ingredients and dissolve in 1 litre of boiled and cooled water.

Because digesting food requires water, always try and drink with your meals. If you have limited water, limit your food intake or even think of not eating at all. Remember: you'll die from dehydration more quickly than from starvation.

PERSONAL HYGIENE

In any situation, cleanliness is an important factor in preventing infection and disease. It becomes even more important in a survival situation. Poor hygiene can reduce your chances of living.

A daily shower with hot water and soap is ideal, but if water is scarce, take an 'air' bath. Remove as much of your clothing as practical and expose your body to the sun and air for at least an hour. Be careful not to burn.

If you don't have soap, use ashes or sand, or make soap from animal fat and wood ashes, if your situation allows. To make soap:

- Extract grease from animal fat by cutting the fat into small pieces and cooking them in a pot.
- Add enough water to the pot to keep the fat from sticking as it cooks.
- Cook the fat slowly, stirring frequently.
- After the fat is rendered, pour the grease into a container to harden.
- Place ashes in a container with a spout near the bottom.
- Pour water over the ashes and collect the liquid that drips out of the spout in a separate container. This liquid is the potash or lye. Another way to get the lye is to pour the slurry (the mixture of ashes and water) through a straining cloth.

- In a cooking pot, mix two parts grease to one part potash.
- Place this mixture over a fire and boil it until it thickens.

After the soap mixture cools, you can use it in the semi-liquid state directly from the pot. You can also pour it into a pan, allow it to harden, and cut it into bars for later use.

KEEP YOUR HANDS CLEAN

Germs on your hands can infect food and wounds. Wash your hands after handling any material that is likely to carry germs, after visiting the latrine, and before handling any food, food utensils or drinking water. Keep your fingernails closely trimmed and clean. Keep your fingers out of your mouth.

KEEP YOUR HAIR CLEAN

Your hair can become a haven for bacteria or fleas, lice, and other parasites. Keeping your hair clean, combed and trimmed helps you avoid this danger.

KEEP YOUR CLOTHING CLEAN

Keep your clothing and bedding as clean as possible to reduce the chance of skin infection as well as decrease the danger of parasitic infestation. Clean your outer clothing whenever it becomes soiled. Wear clean underclothing and socks each day. If water is scarce, 'air'-clean your clothing by shaking, airing and sunning it for two hours. If you are using a sleeping bag, turn it inside out after each use, fluff it, and air it.

KEEP YOUR TEETH CLEAN

Thoroughly clean your mouth and teeth with a toothbrush at least once each day. If you don't have a toothbrush, make a chewing stick. Find a twig about 20 cm long and a centimetre wide. Chew one end of the stick to separate the fibres. Now brush your teeth thoroughly. Another method is to wrap a clean strip of cloth around your fingers and rub your teeth with it to wipe away food particles. You can also brush your teeth with small amounts of sand, baking soda, salt or soap. Then rinse your mouth with water, salt water or willow bark tea. Also, flossing your teeth with string or fibre helps oral hygiene.

If you have cavities, you can make temporary fillings by placing candle wax, tobacco, aspirin, hot pepper, toothpaste or powder, or portions of a ginger root into the cavity. Make sure you clean the cavity by rinsing or picking the particles out before placing a filling in the cavity.

TAKE CARE OF YOUR FEET

My brother, who was in the Paras, developed septicaemia just twelve hours after picking up a blister on exercises.

If you get a small blister, do not open it – an intact blister is safe from infection. Apply a padding material around the blister to relieve pressure and reduce friction. If the blister bursts, treat it as an open wound: clean and dress it daily and pad around it.

Leave large blisters intact. To avoid having the blister burst or tear under pressure and cause a painful and open sore, do the following. You'll need a needle and a clean or sterilized thread.

- Clean the blister, then run the needle and thread through it.
- Detach the needle leaving both ends of the thread hanging out of the blister. The thread will absorb the liquid inside. This reduces the size of the hole and ensures it does not close up.
- Pad around the area.

> **in a survival situation you must control serious bleeding immediately, the victim can die within a matter of minutes**

LIMITED TRAUMA

Any one of the following can cause airway obstruction, resulting in death.

- Foreign matter in mouth of throat that obstructs the opening to the trachea.
- Face or neck injuries.
- Inflammation and swelling of mouth or throat caused by inhaling smoke, flames or irritating vapours or by an allergic reaction.

- 'Kink' in the throat (caused by the neck bent forward so that the chin rests upon the chest) blocking the passage of air.
- Tongue blocks passage of air to the lungs upon unconsciousness. When an individual is unconscious, the muscles of the lower jaw and tongue relax as the neck drops forward, causing the lower jaw to sag and the tongue to drop back and block the passage of air.

Severe Bleeding

Severe bleeding from any major vessel in the body is extremely dangerous. The loss of one litre of blood will produce moderate symptoms of shock. The loss of two litres will produce a severe state of shock that places the body in extreme danger. The loss of three is usually fatal.

Shock

Shock is not a disease in itself. It's a clinical condition that arises when cardiac output is too small to fill the arteries with blood under enough pressure. As a result, it cannot provide an adequate blood supply to the organ and tissues.

LIFE-SAVING TECHNIQUES

Control panic. Be calm and reassuring.

Perform a rapid physical examination. Look for the cause of the injury and follow the ABCs of first aid, (Airways, Breathing, Circulation), starting with the airway and breathing, but be discerning. A person may die from arterial bleeding more quickly than from an airway obstruction in some cases.

OPEN AIRWAY AND MAINTAIN

You can open an airway and maintain it by observing the following:
- Check whether the victim has a partial or complete airway obstruction. If he can cough or speak, allow him to clear the obstruction naturally. Stand by, reassure the victim, and be ready to clear his airway and perform mouth-to-mouth resuscitation should he become unconscious. If his airway is completely obstructed, administer abdominal thrusts until the obstruction is cleared.
- Using a finger, quickly sweep the victim's mouth clear of any foreign objects, broken teeth, dentures, sand.

- Use the jaw thrust method: grasp the angles of the victim's lower jaw and lift with both hands, one on each side, moving the jaw forward. For stability, rest your elbows on the surface on which the victim is lying. If his lips are closed, gently open the lower lip with your thumb.

CONTROL BLEEDING

In a survival situation you must control serious bleeding immediately because replacement fluids are not normally available and the victim can die within a matter of minutes. External bleeding falls into the following classifications (according to its source):

- *Arterial.* A cut artery issues *bright red* blood from the wound in *distinct spurts* or pulses that correspond to the rhythm of the heartbeat. Because the blood is being forced out under pressure, you can lose most blood this way, so treat the wound quickly.
- *Venous.* A steady flow of *dark red, maroon, or bluish blood* characterises bleeding from a vein. More easily controlled than arterial bleeding.
- *Capillary.* The capillaries are the extremely small vessels that connect the arteries with the veins. Capillary bleeding most commonly occurs in minor cuts and scrapes. This type of bleeding is not difficult to control.

You can control external bleeding by direct pressure, indirect pressure (pressure points) elevation, digital ligation, or tourniquet.

DIRECT PRESSURE

The most effective way to control external bleeding is by applying pressure directly over the wound. This pressure must not only be firm enough to stop the bleeding, but it must also be maintained long enough to 'seal off' the damaged surface.

If bleeding continues after having applied direct pressure for thirty minutes, apply a pressure dressing. This dressing consists of a thick wad of gauze or other suitable material applied directly over the wound and held in place with a tightly wrapped bandage. It should be tighter than an ordinary compression bandage but not so tight that it impairs circulation to the rest of the limb. Once you apply the dressing, *do not remove it,* even when the dressing becomes blood soaked.

Leave the pressure dressing in place for one or two days, after which you can remove and replace it with a smaller dressing.

In the long-term survival environment, make fresh, daily dressing changes and inspect for signs of infection.

ELEVATION

Raising an injured limb as high as possible above the heart's level slows blood loss. However, elevation alone will not control bleeding entirely; you must also apply direct pressure over the wound.

When treating a snakebite, however, keep the extremity lower than the heart.

> " if you do not have antibiotics and the wound has become severely infected, consider maggot therapy, despite its hazards "

PRESSURE POINTS

You can find pressure points where main arteries lie near the surface of the skin or they pass over a bony prominence. You can use finger pressure on a pressure point to slow arterial bleeding until the application of a pressure dressing. But remember, pressure point control is not as effective for controlling bleeding as direct pressure exerted on the wound.

If you cannot remember the exact location of the pressure points, follow this rule: apply pressure at the end of the joint just above the injured area. On hands, feet, and head, this will be the wrist, ankle, and neck, respectively.

DIGITAL LIGATION

This is the medical term for pressing down with a finger on the severed vein or artery. Maintain the pressure until the bleeding stops or slows down enough to apply a pressure bandage, attempt elevation, and so forth.

TOURNIQUET

Use a tourniquet only when direct pressure over the bleeding point and all other methods have failed. If you leave a tourniquet in place too long, the damage to the tissues can lead to gangrene, and loss of the limb. An improperly applied tourniquet can also cause permanent damage to nerves and other tissues at the site of the constriction.

If you must use a tourniquet, place it around the extremity, between the wound and the heart, 5-10 cm above the wound site. Never place it directly over the wound or a fracture. Use a stick as a handle to tighten the tourniquet and tighten it only enough to stop blood flow. When you have tightened the tourniquet, bind the free end of the stick to the limb to prevent unwinding.

After securing the tourniquet, clean and bandage the wound. A lone survivor *does not* remove or release an applied tourniquet. In a buddy system, however, the buddy can release the tourniquet pressure every ten to fifteen minutes for a minute or so to let blood flow to the rest of the extremity and avoid limb loss.

PREVENT AND TREAT SHOCK

Anticipate shock following all injuries. Treat all injured people as follows, regardless of their symptoms.

- If the victim is conscious, place him on a level surface with the lower extremities elevated 15-20 cm.
- If the victim is unconscious, place him on his side or abdomen with his head turned to one side to prevent choking on vomit, blood or other fluids.
- If you are unsure of the best position, place the victim flat on his front, face to the side with mouth open.
- Maintain body heat by insulating the victim from the surroundings and, in some instances, applying external heat.
- If wet, remove all the victim's wet clothing as soon as possible and replace with dry clothing.
- Improvise a shelter to insulate the victim from the weather.
- Use warm liquids or foods, a pre-warmed sleeping bag, another person, warmed water in canteens, hot rocks wrapped in clothing, or

fires on either side of the victim to provide external warmth.

• If the victim is conscious, slowly administer small doses of a warm salt or sugar solution, if available. (see chapter on water).

• If the victim is unconscious or has abdominal wounds, do not give fluids by mouth.

• Let the victim rest for at least twenty-four hours. Reassess the victim constantly.

• If you are a lone survivor, lie in a depression in the ground, behind a tree, or any other place out of the weather, with your head lower than your feet.

WOUNDS

A wound is any injury that breaks the skin. Examples include open wounds, skin diseases, frostbite, trenchfoot and burns.

OPEN WOUNDS

In a survival situation open wounds are serious for two reasons: tissue damage and blood loss from the wound itself, and the risk of infection. Bacteria on the object that made the wound, on the individual's skin and clothing, or on other foreign material or dirt that touches the wound may cause infection.

Clean the wound as soon as possible after it occurs by:

• removing or cutting clothing away from it

• looking for an exit wound if a sharp object, gunshot or projectile caused a wound

• thoroughly cleaning the skin around the wound

• rinsing (not scrubbing) the wound with large amounts of water under pressure. You can use fresh urine if water is not available.

The 'open treatment' method is the safest way to manage wounds in survival situations. Do *not* try to close any wound by suturing or similar procedures; leave it open to allow pus to drain away. As long as the wound can drain it generally will not become life-threatening, regardless of how unpleasant it looks or smells.

Cover the wound with a clean dressing. Place a bandage on the dressing to hold it in place. Change the dressing daily to check for infection.

If a wound is gaping, you can bring the edges together with adhesive tape cut in the form of a 'butterfly' or 'dumb-bell'.

In a survival situation, some degree of wound infection is almost inevitable. Pain, swelling, and redness around the wound, increased temperature, and pus in the wound or on the dressing indicate that infection is present.

To treat an infected wound:

• Place a warm, moist compress directly on the infected wound. Change the compress when it cools, keeping a warm compress on the wound for a total of 30 minutes. Apply the compresses three or four times daily.

• Drain the wound. Open and gently probe the infected wound with a sterile instrument.

• Dress and bandage the wound.

• Drink a lot of water.

Continue this treatment daily until all signs of infection have disappeared. If you do not have antibiotics and the wound has become severely infected, does not heal, and ordinary cleaning is impossible, consider maggot therapy, despite its hazards:

• Expose the wound to flies for one day and then cover it.

• Check daily for maggots.

• Once maggots develop, keep wound covered but check daily.

• Remove all maggots when they have cleaned out all dead tissue and before they start on healthy tissue. Increased pain and bright red blood in the wound indicate that the maggots have reached healthy tissue.

• Flush the wound repeatedly with sterile water or fresh urine to remove the maggots.

• Check the wound every four hours for several days to ensure all maggots have been removed.

• Bandage the wound and treat it as any other wound. It should heal normally.

You could also try these natural remedies:

- *Garlic.* Boil and use the water.
- *Salt water.* Use two or three tablespoons of salt per litre of water – the solution will kill bacteria.
- *Bee honey.* Use it straight or dissolved in water.
- *Sphagnum moss.* Found in boggy areas worldwide, it is a natural source of iodine. Use as a dressing.

BONE AND JOINT INJURY

In a survival situation you could face bone and joint injuries that include fractures, dislocations and sprains.

FRACTURES

There are basically two types of fracture: open and closed. With an open (or compound) fracture, the bone protrudes through the skin and complicates the actual fracture with an open wound. After setting the fracture, treat the wound as any other open wound.

The closed fracture has no open wounds. Follow the rules for immobilization, and set and splint the fracture.

The signs and symptoms of a fracture are pain, tenderness, discoloration, swelling deformity, loss of function, and grating (a sound or feeling that occurs when broken bone ends rub together).

The dangers with a fracture are the severing or compression of a nerve or blood vessel at the site of fracture. For this reason minimum manipulation should be done, and then only very cautiously. If you notice the area below the break becoming numb, swollen, cool to the touch, or turning pale, and the victim shows signs of shock, a major vessel may have been severed. You must control this internal bleeding. Treat the victim for shock, and replace lost fluids.

Often it is necessary to maintain traction during the splinting and healing process. You can effectively pull smaller bones such as those in the arm or lower leg by hand. You can create traction by wedging a hand or foot in the V-notch of a tree and pushing against the tree with the other extremity. You can then splint the break.

Very strong muscles hold a broken thighbone (femur) in place making it difficult to maintain traction during healing. You can make an improvised traction splint using natural material.

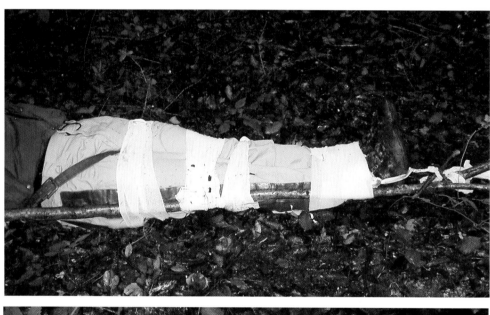

- Get two forked branches or saplings at least 5 cm in diameter. Measure one from the patient's armpit to 30 cm past his unbroken leg. Measure the other from the groin to 30 cm past the unbroken leg. Ensure that both extend an equal distance beyond the end of the leg.
- Pad the two splints. Notch the ends without forks and lash a 20–30 cm cross member made from a 5 cm diameter branch between them.
- Using available material (e.g. vines, cloth, rawhide), tie the splint around the upper portion of the body and down the length of the broken leg. Follow the splinting rules.
- With available material, fashion a wrap that will extend around the ankle, with the two free ends tied to the cross member.
- Place a 10–2.5 cm stick in the middle of the free ends of the ankle wrap between the cross member and the foot. Using the stick, twist the material to make the traction easier.
- Continue twisting until the broken leg is as long or slightly longer than the unbroken leg.
- Lash the stick to maintain traction.

Note: Over time you may lose traction because the material weakens – check the traction periodically. If you must change or repair the splint, maintain the traction manually for a short time.

DISLOCATIONS

Dislocations are the separations of bone joints causing the bones to go out of proper alignment. These misalignments can be extremely painful and can cause an impairment of nerves or circulation below the area affected. You must place these joints back

into alignment as quickly as possible.

Signs and symptoms of dislocations are joint pain, tenderness, swelling, discoloration, limited range of motion, and deformity of the joint. You treat dislocations by reduction, immobilization, and rehabilitation.

Reduction or 'setting' requires placing the bones back into their proper alignment. You can use several methods, but manual traction or the use of weights to pull the bones are the safest and easiest. Once performed, reduction decreases the victim's pain and allows for normal function and circulation. Without an X-ray, you can judge proper alignment by the look and feel of the joint and by comparing it to the joint on the opposite side.

Immobilization is nothing more than splinting the dislocation after reduction. You can use any field-expedient material for a splint or you can splint an extremity to the body. The basic guidelines for splinting are:

- Splint above and below the fracture site.
- Pad splints to reduce discomfort.
- Check circulation below the fracture after making each tie on the splint.

To rehabilitate the dislocation, remove the splints after one or two weeks. Gradually use the injured joint until fully healed.

SPRAINS

The accidental overstretching of a tendon or ligament causes a sprain. The signs and symptoms are pain, swelling, tenderness and discoloration (black and blue).

When treating sprains, think RICE:

R – Rest injured area.

I – Ice for twenty-four hours, then heat after that.

C – Compression-wrap and/or splint to help stabilize. If possible, leave the boot on a sprained ankle unless circulation is compromised.

E – Elevate the affected area.

> **inspect your body at least once a day to ensure there are no insects attached to you. If you find ticks attached to your body, cover them with tree sap to cut off their air supply.**

INSECTS

Insects and related pests are hazards in a survival situation. They not only cause irritations, but they are often carriers of diseases that cause severe allergic reactions in some individuals.

Ticks transmit Lyme disease and Rocky Mountain spotted fever–common in many parts of the United States.

Mosquitoes may carry malaria, dengue and other diseases.

Flies can carry disease from contact with infectious sources, spreading sleeping sickness, typhoid, cholera and dysentery.

Fleas can transmit plague.

Lice can transmit typhus and relapsing fever.

The best way to avoid the complications of insect bites and stings is to keep immunizations (including booster shots) up to date, avoid insect-infested areas, use netting and insect repellent, and wear all clothing properly.

If you get bitten or stung, do not scratch the bite or sting.

Inspect your body at least once a day to ensure there are no insects attached to you. If you find ticks attached to your body, cover them with a substance such as Vaseline, heavy oil or tree sap to cut off their air supply. Without air, the tick releases its hold and you can remove it. Take care to remove the whole tick. Use tweezers if you have them. Grasp the tick where the mouth parts are attached to the skin. Do not squeeze the tick's body. Wash your hands after touching the tick. Clean the wound daily until healed.

BEE AND WASP STINGS

If stung by a bee, immediately remove the stinger and venom sac, if attached, by scraping with a fingernail or a knife blade. Do not squeeze or grasp the stinger or venom sac, as squeezing will force more venom into the wound. Wash the sting site thoroughly with soap and water to lessen the chance of a secondary infection.

If you know or suspect that you are allergic to insect stings, always carry an insect sting kit with you.

Relieve the itching and discomfort caused by insect bites by applying:

- Cold compresses
- A cooling paste of mud and ashes
- Sap from dandelions
- Coconut meat
- Crushed cloves of garlic
- Onion

SPIDER BITES AND SCORPION STINGS

Black widow, funnel-web spider and scorpion: treat for shock. Clean and dress the bite area to reduce the risk of infection. An anti-venom is available.

The brown house spider or brown recluse spider is a small, light brown spider identified by a dark brown violin shape on its back. There is no pain or so little pain, that usually a victim is not aware of the bite. Within a few hours a painful red area with a mottled cyanotic (bluish blood) centre appears. Necrosis (tissue death) does not occur in all bites, but usually in three to four days, a star-shaped, firm area of deep purple discoloration appears at the bite site. The area turns dark in a week or two, then the margins separate and the scab falls off, leaving an open ulcer. Secondary infection and regional swollen lymph glands usually become visible at this stage. The outstanding characteristic of the brown recluse bite is an ulcer that does not heal but persists for weeks or months. In addition to the ulcer, there is often a systemic reaction that is serious and may lead to death. Reactions (fever, chills, joint pain, vomiting, and a generalized rash) may occur, chiefly in children or debilitated persons.

Tarantulas are large, hairy spiders found mainly in the tropics. Most do not inject venom, but some South American species do. They have large fangs. If bitten, pain and bleeding are certain, and infection is likely. Treat a tarantula bite as any open wound, and try to prevent infection. If symptoms of poisoning appear, treat as for the bite of the black widow spider.

Scorpions are all poisonous to a greater or lesser degree. There are two different reactions, depending on the species:

• Severe local reaction only, with pain and swelling around the area of the sting. Possible prickly sensation around the mouth and a thick-feeling tongue.

• Severe systemic reaction, with little or no visible local reaction. Local pain may be present. Systemic reaction includes respiratory difficulties, thick-feeling tongue, body spasms, drooling, gastric distention, double vision, blindness, involuntary rapid movement of the eyeballs, involuntary urination and defecation, and heart failure. Death is rare, occurring mainly in children and adults with high blood pressure or illnesses.

Treat scorpion stings as you would a black widow bite.

SNAKEBITES

The chance of a snakebite in a survival situation is rather small, if you are familiar with the various types of snakes and their habitats. However, it could happen and you should know how to treat a snakebite. Deaths from snakebites are rare. More than half of snakebite victims have little or no poisoning, and only about a quarter develop serious systemic poisoning. However, the chance of a snakebite in a survival situation can affect morale, and failure to take preventive measures or to treat a snakebite properly can result in needless tragedy.

The primary concern in the treatment of snakebite is to limit the amount

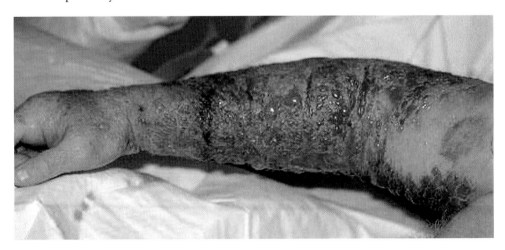

> **symptoms of a poisonous snake bite may be spontaneous bleeding, bloodin the urine, pain at the site of the bite, and swelling at the site of the bite within a few minutes**

of eventual tissue destruction around the bite area.

A bite wound, regardless of the type of animal that inflicted it, can become infected from bacteria in the animal's mouth. With non-poisonous as well as poisonous snakebites, this local infection is responsible for a large part of the residual damage that results.

Snake venoms not only contain poisons that attack the victim's central nervous system (neurotoxins) and blood circulation (haemotoxins), but also digestive enzymes (cytotoxins) to aid in digesting their prey. These poisons can cause a very large area of tissue death (necrosis), leaving a large open wound. This condition could lead to the need for eventual amputation if not treated.

Shock and panic in a person bitten by a snake can also affect the person's recovery. Excitement, hysteria and panic can speed up the circulation, causing the body to absorb the toxin quickly. Signs of shock occur within the first thirty minutes after the bite.

Before you start treating a snakebite, determine whether the snake was poisonous or non-poisonous. Bites from a non-poisonous snake will show rows of teeth. Bites from a poisonous snake may have rows of teeth showing, but will have one or more distinctive puncture marks caused by fang penetration. Symptoms of a poisonous bite may be spontaneous bleeding from the nose and anus, blood in the urine, pain at the site of the bite, and swelling at the site of the bite within a few minutes or up to two hours later.

Breathing difficulty, paralysis, weakness, twitching and numbness are also signs of neurotoxic venoms. These signs usually appear within two hours after the bite.

If you determine that a poisonous snake bit an individual, take the following steps:

- Reassure the victim and keep him still.
- Set up for shock and force fluids or give an intravenous drip.
- Remove watches, rings, bracelets, or other constricting items.
- Clean the bite area.
- Maintain an airway (especially if bitten near the face or neck) and be prepared to administer mouth-to-mouth resuscitation or CPR (Cardio pulmonary resuscitation).
- Use a constricting band between the wound and the heart.
- Immobilize the site.
- Remove the poison as soon as possible by using a mechanical suction device or by squeezing.

Do not:

Give the victim alcoholic beverages or tobacco products.

Give morphine or other central nervous system (CNS) depressors.

Make any deep cuts at the bite site. Cutting opens capillaries that in turn open a direct route into the bloodstream for venom and infection.

Put your hands on your face or rub your eyes, as venom may be on your hands. Venom may cause blindness.

Break open the large blisters that form around the bite site.

After caring for the victim as above, take the following actions to minimize local effects:

- If infection appears, keep the wound open and clean – soap will suffice.
- Use heat after 24-48 hours to help prevent the spread of local infection. Heat also helps to draw out an infection.
- Keep the wound covered with a dry, sterile dressing.
- Have the victim drink large amounts of fluids until the infection is gone.

SKIN DISEASES AND AILMENTS

Although boils, fungal infections and rashes rarely develop into a serious health problem, they cause discomfort and you should treat them. Use the natural remedies listed above in the section on wounds.

BOILS

Apply warm compresses to bring the boil to a head. Then open the boil using a sterile knife, wire, needle or similar item. Thoroughly clean out the pus using soap and water. Cover the boil site, checking it periodically to ensure no further infection develops.

FUNGAL INFECTIONS

Keep the skin clean and dry, and expose the infected area to as much sunlight as possible. *Do not scratch* the affected area. On active duty in tropical regions, guys in the Regiment use anti-fungal powders, lye soap, chlorine bleach, alcohol, vinegar, concentrated saltwater and iodine to treat fungal infections, with varying degrees of success.

RASHES

To treat a skin rash effectively, first determine what is causing it, then follow these rules:
* don't scratch
* keep moist rashes dry
* keep dry rashes moist.

To dry weeping rashes make a compress of vinegar or tannic acid derived from tea, or from boiling acorns or the bark of a hardwood tree. Moisten dry rashes by rubbing on small amounts of animal fat you've saved from cooking.

TRENCH-FOOT

This happens when feet are wet and cold in near-freezing conditions for a long time. Keep your feet dry: dry your wet socks against your body and put them on after washing your feet daily.

GASTROINTESTINAL ILLNESS

Gastroenteritis and dehydration. Gastroenteritis is still a killer in the third world, especially for young children (I include typhoid, cholera, giardia, salmonella, 'food poisoning', etc. under the general heading gastroenteritis). The most important action you can take in preventing gastroenteritis is to wash your hands following defecation. All drinking water should be boiled unless you are sure of its purity. Hand washing and clean water will prevent 99 per cent of diarrhoeal disease.

DIARRHOEA

Commonly caused by a change of water and food, drinking contaminated water, eating spoiled food, becoming fatigued and using dirty dishes. Prevention is the best cure but try one of the following treatments if you're unlucky:

- Limit your intake of fluids for 24 hours.
- Drink one cup of a strong tea solution every two hours until the diarrhoea slows or stops. The tannic acid in the tea helps to control the diarrhoea. Boil the inner bark of a hardwood tree for two hours or more to release the tannic acid.
- Make a solution of one handful of ground chalk, charcoal, or dried bones in treated water. Citrus fruit rinds make it more effective. Take two tablespoons of the solution every two hours until the diarrhoea slows or stops.

INTESTINAL PARASITES

To avoid worm infestations and other intestinal parasites, never go barefoot and avoid uncooked meat and raw vegetables contaminated by raw sewage (including human faeces used as a fertilizer). If you are unlucky, try one of the following. If it doesn't work, try another.

- *Salt water.* Dissolve four tablespoons of salt in one litre of water and drink. Do not repeat this treatment.
- *Tobacco.* Eat one or two cigarettes. The nicotine in the cigarette will kill or stun the worms long enough for your system to pass them. If the infestation is severe, repeat the treatment after 24 or 48 hours, *but no sooner.*
- *Kerosene.* Drink two tablespoons of kerosene *but no more.* If necessary, you can repeat this treatment after 24 or 48 hours. Be careful not to inhale the fumes; they may cause lung irritation.
- *Hot peppers.* You can eat them raw or put them in soups or rice and meat dishes. They won't cure you but they will help stop worms getting attached.

BURNS

Follow these steps to relieve pain, help speed healing, and protect against infection:

- Soak dressings or clean rags for ten minutes in a boiling tannic acid solution (obtained from tea, inner bark of hardwood trees, or acorns boiled in water).
- Cool the dressings or clean rags and apply over burns.
- Treat as an open wound.
- Replace fluid loss.
- Maintain airway.
- Treat for shock.
- Consider using morphine, unless the burns are near the face.

ENVIRONMENTAL INJURIES

Heatstroke, hypothermia, frostbite and altitude sickness are environmental injuries you could face.

HEATSTROKE

The breakdown of the body's heat regulatory system, which keeps your temperature rising above 40.5C, causes heatstroke. It can strike out of the blue without a build-up of symptoms such as cramps or dehydration.

Typical symptoms are:
- swollen, bright-red face
- whites of eyes going red
- lack of sweat
- unconsciousness or delirium accompanied by bluish lips and nail beds and cool skin.

Cool the victim as rapidly as possible by dipping in a cool stream or dousing with any liquid, including urine. At the very least, wet the victim's head, and apply cool, wet compresses to all the joints, especially the neck, armpits and crotch. Fan them. Treat for dehydration with lightly salted water.

Expect, during cooling:

- vomiting
- diarrhoea
- struggling
- shivering
- shouting
- prolonged unconsciousness
- rebound heatstroke within 48 hours
- cardiac arrest – be ready to perform CPR.

HYPOTHERMIA

Defined as the body's failure to maintain a temperature of 36C. Exposure to cool or cold temperatures over a short or long time can cause hypothermia. Dehydration and lack of food and rest predispose the survivor to hypothermia.

Unlike heatstroke, you must gradually warm the hypothermia victim. Get the victim into dry clothing and out of the wind. Replace lost fluids, and warm him.

FROSTBITE

This injury results from frozen tissues. Light frostbite involves only the skin which takes on a dull, whitish pallor. Deep frostbite extends to a depth below the skin. The tissues become solid and immovable. Your feet, hands and exposed facial areas are particularly vulnerable to frostbite.

When with others, prevent frostbite by using the buddy system. Check your buddy's face often and make sure that he checks yours. If you are alone, periodically cover your nose and the lower part of your face with your mittens.

Do not try to thaw the affected areas by placing them close to an open flame. Gently rub them in lukewarm water. Dry the areas and place them next to your skin to warm them at body temperature.

ALTITUDE SICKNESS

This tends to strike above 2000 m and affects almost half the number of people who climb above 3000 m. It is caused by fluid build up in the brain or in the lungs. Symptoms include loss of appetite, dizziness, a tendency to urinate a lot and nausea. You can also wake up in the night feeling that you are suffocating. Take it seriously and act quickly, because it is a killer.

You can reduce the risk of altitude sickness by ascending slowly at a rate of 300 m per day. Acclimatize particularly carefully between 2,500 and 3000 m.

To cure, try to get below 2,000 m before nightfall, as sleeping at high altitudes can exacerbate the problem. Even dropping 500 m can work.

> " take altitude sickness seriously and act quickly, because it is a killer "

VITAMIN DEFICIENCIES

Vitamin deficiency takes a long time to kick in – weeks probably, maybe even months – but it's worth knowing the symptoms so you can try and take steps to remedy it.

Scurvy is caused by a lack of vitamin C. Your blood vessels weaken, leading to easy bruising and bleeding gums. Teeth become sore, joints swollen and you lose your appetite. Cure by eating foods rich in vitamin C: citrus fruits, lettuce, celery, onions, carrots, potatoes. Pine needle tea is also very rich in this essential vitamin.

Beriberi is caused by a lack of vitamin B1, or thiamine. You grow weak, your legs stiffen and movement becomes painful or impossible. First seen in people whose diet relied too heavily on refined rice, it can be cured quickly by thiamine injections or eating cereals, legumes, meat, milk and fruit.

Pellagra is caused by a lack of niacin – another component of vitamin B. Symptoms include weakness, insomnia, mouth sores and skin cracking and developing scales in sunlight. It can lead on to diarrhoea and other stomach and gut complaints. Milk, meat, fish, wholegrain cereals and vegetables contain the niacin necessary to cure it.

CHAPTER FOURTEEN

GETTING FOUND

Signalling and rescue: the best way to get rescued is to prepare for it. You should always let someone at the end point of a journey know when you are supposed to be arriving and where you set out from. This means they can react to good purpose if you fail to arrive - in effect, you've given them a point of departure and a bearing to follow.

This is a good habit to get into whether you are setting out from a B&B in the Cairngorms for a walk in the mountains or about to cross a bit of Australian outback during the holiday of a lifetime.

I've never run the figures but it's my belief that potential disaster is never more than a couple of hours away – wherever you are in the world.

You can increase your chances of being found by applying some pretty basic logic and commonsense. If you know you're venturing into dangerous terrain, hire a satellite phone (see chapter on Equipment). Failing that, make sure your mobile phone is charged up. You never know: you may be able to get a signal. In most conditions bright colours show up better than dark ones and while a fluorescent orange sleeping bag may make your eyeballs wince and not seem very 'green', it could save your life. So throw fashion to the wind and forget about your dreams of becoming at one with mother nature. Prepare your equipment to be seen or you might find yourself merging with nature – fatally.

ON THE MOVE

You're obviously going to be heading for civilization, so follow roads but also pipelines, telegraph wires and electricity pylons. Knowing which way to go might be a problem so, short of an arrow telling you, look for markers that might give distances to towns, or wait until dark and to see if any lights show up on the horizon.

When you are breaking camp, leave clear indications of your intentions and direction of travel. There are some near universal signs for this.

Direction indicators: arrows made out of stones and pebbles; a pile of rocks with a small rock left at a distance from it to show direction; a pointer in a forked stick stuck into the ground; a forked stick laid on the ground; arrows cut into bark.

If the path forks on your journey, indicate which way you are going with an arrow and 'block' the alternative route with a two crossed sticks or a line of three stuck into the ground.

Bear in mind search patterns and the fact that rescuers will try to think their way into your mindset. Therefore if the weather is foul, they will expect you to head for shelter, such as the lee of a hill. If you find a very obvious piece of shelter, the chances are the search party will find it too so leave some sort of message or indicator there before you move on.

SEARCH PARTIES

If your route is known, a methodical search party will probably move across it in a regular pattern, trying to adapt to your behaviour.

——————— search pattern

——————▶ your expected route

x marks your suspected location
Fan shows search pattern

An air search will follow the top pattern on flat ground or perform a box crawl for a missing aircraft, for example.

plane ——— your route ——————▶

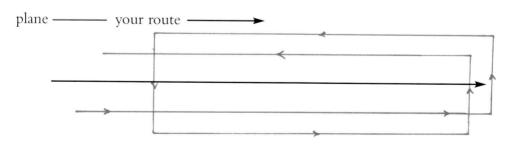

Over hills and mountains, a thorough contour search from the air will sweep down slopes and go up and down valleys.

SIGNALS

It will quickly become apparent to you which signals are most appropriate in any given situation.

The international distress call for mountaineers is six blasts on your whistle in quick succession, followed by a minute's silence, and then repeated. This saves you having to keep up a barrage of sound. If anyone on a mountain hears a whistle, they will wait to see if the pattern occurs.

This can be applied to flashing lights – a torch for example, or shouts.

As widely known is the famous SOS call: ... – – – ... This can be sounded out, flashed, even cut into sand, snow or turf.

SATELLITE PHONES, MOBILE PHONES AND RADIO TRANSMITTERS

Many people have been saved by their mobile phones. Boaters who were wrecked off Australia even managed to text back to England, where people notified the Australian authorities.

As I've said earlier, I'm a great believer in technology where it's effective, and there are now devices on the market that can bring help quickly and accurately.

Each works differently but there are a few things to remember.

Battery power is precious, so do not keep the thing on all the time. Time your transmissions to short bursts but keep them regular, so listeners can pick up a pattern.

Cold makes batteries weak, but heat revives them. So if your battery seems dead, it's worthwhile trying to warm it up and trying again.

Satellite phones can be life-savers. In fact, if we'd had them in the first Gulf War, the whole story of Bravo Two Zero would have been different. We could have phoned in, got picked up and lived to fight another day as a unit. During the filming of *Hunting Chris Ryan*, I used mine extensively.

Small emergency transmitters can be found in some survival equipment.

They send out bleeps that allow rescuers to get a fix on you, but bear in mind they will have a limited range and battery life. If there is no sign of rescue when you go down, switch the device off until you think help might be approaching.

Some walkie-talkies cannot transmit around obstacles – they need clear air between them. If there is a radio, learn how to use it. Shouting 'Mayday Mayday' will only get you so far. Make sure you are being clear and precise when you give instructions, and listen to theirs. If you think reception is too poor for clear voice communications and you know morse code, try tapping a short message on the microphone.

If asked to spell out a word, use the international phonetic alphabet:

A – Alpha	**J** – Juliet	**S** – Sierra
B – Bravo	**K** – Kilo	**T** – Tango
C – Charlie	**L** – Lima	**U** – Uniform
D – Delta	**M** – Mike	**V** – Victor
E – Echo	**N** – November	**W** – Whisky
F – Foxtrot	**O** – Oscar	**X** – X-ray
G – Golf	**P** – Papa	**Y** – Yankee
H – Hotel	**Q** – Quebec	**Z** – Zulu
I – India	**R** – Romeo	

FIRES

If you remember the visibility rule, knowing which sort of fire to build should be simple. Against dark backgrounds make white smoke, against pale backgrounds make dark smoke, and at night make flames.

Whatever you do, watch out for bush fires.

Building a signal fire should be a high priority and once built, it must be maintained with dry kindling and the right smoke-making material. If you have enough materials, build three in a triangle.

A pyramid fire fits the bill. It lights quickly, burns fast and can be maintained without too much trouble. Build the pyramid out of three uprights as high as you can make them – two metres would be ideal. Lash a platform half a metre above the ground and build fire on this. Protect it with tarpaulin, or, if you don't have this, with brushwood and branches. The aim is to keep the heart of the fire both dry and ready to light at a moment's notice.

For a supercharged start, you could try the old aerosol flame-thrower trick, but this is highly dangerous and you must weigh the benefits of getting the fire to light quickly against the risk of blowing your hand off. If you part-bury the aerosol in the ground close to the fire, you can aim it, depress the button with a rock, light and stand well back.

In a forest, only white smoke shows up. Fortunately burning leaves make white smoke, but be certain to make sure the fire is hot enough to burn them. If you cannot build your fire in a clearing, see if you can build it in an actual tree. Put kindling in the branches to get a good start.

In the desert and against snow, only black smoke shows up – so burn tyres and oil. Foam rubber from seats will probably be impregnated with flame retardant chemicals, but are worth a try if shredded.

At night, you want huge flames and lots of sparks: dried branches with dried leaves on them will do the trick, but use anything that burns.

In the rainforest, the near impenetrable canopy might trap smoke, so you will need to build a big one. Think of keeping a fire raft in preparation so you can take advantage of the clear space over a river. On a raft, build a raised platform and set your fire on this before allowing it to drift into the middle of the stream. A line of small fire rafts will make more of an impact than a single large one and be more of a practical proposition.

GROUND MARKINGS

Two things to remember: make them stand out against the background and make them big enough – each symbol 10 m long and 3 m wide, for example. The bigger they are, the clearer they will be seen from farther away.

On a beach, use stones and seaweed for greatest effect, but drawing in the sand will show up.

On snow, tramping down an area will show up, but use wreckage if you can or brightly coloured material.

On grassland, try digging up the turf in strips. If you are burning shapes into the grass, be careful the fire doesn't get out of control.

There are some internationally recognized markings that will be read and understood from the air.

SOS – Help (literally: Save Our Souls)

| – injured

X – stuck, unable to move

➤ – have gone this way

N – No or negative

Y or A – Yes or affirmative

△ – safe to land here.

OTHER SYMBOLS

II – need medical supplies
F – need food and water

K – tell me which way to go

□ – need map and compass.

A moving object – even just shaking a blanket or tarpaulin, may attract the eye better than a static symbol.

LIGHTS

Flash SOS or the mountain rescue sign: six flashes in quick succession; wait one minute; six more flashes.

A magnesium block will send out a shower of sparks that can be seen from a surprisingly long distance. So will the flash from your camera.

If you can, make a torch by wrapping an oil or petrol soaked rag around a long stick. Keep it handy for waving around.

SOUNDS

Use SOS or the mountain rescue sign for whistles, shouts, crashes and bangs.

HELIOGRAPH AND MIRRORS

Over 80 per cent of successful air searches have been helped by mirror signalling. Use anything you can: polished metal, glass lenses and old bottles. Scavenge through wreckage or use the wing mirrors on your car. Spend time polishing metal to bring out its shine.

A proper heliograph has a hole in the middle to let you point it accurately, but you can line it up with your eyes as well. The trick is to make it flash, so alter the angle across the target. Practise by making reflected sunlight move across a flat surface a short distance away so you understand angles. When you see the rescue party or vehicle, line it up by putting your free hand between the mirror and the target to make sure you are getting the sun's reflection on to it.

If you are doing this at home, *do not practise on aircraft or drivers.*

FLARES

There are two types of commercial flare: handheld and airborne. Follow the same principles as you would with any other sort of signal and select a colour that will contrast with the background.

Hand flares: hold them away from your body and above your head. When they get too hot to hold, do not drop them in your dinghy, if you are at sea. They will burn through rubber and could set wood on fire.

Airborne flares: pistol-type flares should be fired in a cluster a few seconds apart when you hope rescue is near. Parachute flares last longer and will give rescuers a sense of which direction you are in.

BODY SIGNALS

Use these to communicate with rescuers who are too far off to hear you, or on in any motorized vehicle.

Facing them, both arms raised – pick us up
Facing them, arms at right angles – need mechanical help
Facing them, one arm raised – I'm all right
Facing them, right arm at right angle – will proceed
Facing them, hands on ears – have radio
Facing them, arms straight up, bending from side to side at waist – do not land here
Lying down, arms raised – need medical help
Sideways on, crouched, straight arm moving up and down – drop message
Sideways on, crouched, both arms pointing – land here

HELPING RESCUERS

You can help airborne rescuers by indicating a landing strip and making sure it's safe. It's unlikely that you'll be able to make a landing strip, but what you can do is show where you want supplies to be dropped from a light aircraft.

Helicopters clearly need less space than planes to land, but have their limitations and are vulnerable to sudden crosswinds at landing speeds. They prefer to fly low into the wind before setting down, so bear this in mind if you are clearing a space. Do not pick a spot near power lines or cables – these are hard to see from the air.

A landing space needs to be 30 m in diameter and as level as possible – the gradient should be no more than 1:10. Mark it in the middle with a great big H.

Find a safe place and work out from it: firm ground, no rocks, no low trees or bushes. Stamp down snow or remove as much debris as possible. Set up a windsock nearby.

If you are being winched to safety, let the winch touch the ground first. It is likely to be carrying a strong static electrical charge that you should let earth before touching.

GETTING LOST:

ESCAPE AND EVASION

There may be times when you do not want to be found, and escape and concealment becomes your top priority.

Outside of Hollywood films, pursuers are probably going to be relying solely on two senses: sight and sound. Add scent if they have tracker dogs. Your job then is to make these three senses as useless and irrelevant as possible.

Try and get as much ground between you and your pursuers before they know you are gone. You can move much more quickly if you know they are not looking for you, and the greater the distance between you, the more area they have to clear.

GENERAL

The more care you take, the less chance there is of being caught. Moving quickly makes noise that masks the sound of pursuers and will alert them to your location.

Stay away from habitation, man-made structures, bridges and main roads. Waterways are easily watched from the bank so don't allow for easy escape. Don't be tempted by public transport unless you are confident of blending in, but even if you have the right clothes, be careful – people notice anything out of place. If you've slept in a ditch, you'll look like you've slept in a ditch. If you haven't washed for two days, you'll smell that way.

And keep away from taxis. You never know where you might end up. (I had some friends in the first Gulf conflict that hopped into a taxi and got caught.)

SCENT

There are a few steps that you can take to throw dogs off the trail. Ideally, you want to get the dog confused so that the handler loses faith in it. Once he gets annoyed, the dog will stop performing for him and your chances of evading capture increase.

Water will mask your scent. A trained dog handler will cast around on both sides of a river or stream to try and find out where you have got out, so get out a couple of times and lay a false trail with a ninety degree turn in it before doubling back on your tracks. You can also confuse tracker dogs by deliberately crossing a field with livestock in it and getting as close to them as possible so that their scent masks yours.

If the dogs catch up with you, they may be trained to kill. If that is the case, your only chance is to kill them first. Get a rock, a cosh, a short, fat, heavy stick, or ideally a hammer. Wrap something around your weakest arm – a coat is good – and offer it to the dog when it attacks. As soon as it latches on, try and brain it with the heavy object. Really go for it – you want to crack its skull or break its neck. If that fails, try and poke its eyes out with your fingers, thumbs or a stick.

If it's worrying you while you are on the ground, try and get up, holding an arm across your throat for protection, then try and crack the dog's skull.

However a single dog may not attack if you act passively. Lie on the ground and do not move, even when it pisses on you or gives you a nip. In fact, that's a good sign. It means it thinks the threat is over.

SOUND

Your own sounds will not be so obvious if you are near something else that is making a sound, like a stream. Otherwise, try to move smoothly and carefully, keeping an eye open for obstacles before you meet them. Remember, if your pursuer cannot see you, they will be concentrating on any unfamiliar noise.

As a rule of thumb, the more noise they make, the less chance there is of them hearing you.

SIGHT

Unfortunately, the human eye is tuned to pick up movement. That can help you see them but of course the reverse is true as well.

Travel at night as much as possible. Avoid roads, where you may by spotted without even realizing it, and terrain that leaves obvious tracks, such as snow. Keep to the side of open ground, even if it requires making a detour, but beware of traps. A skilled chase team will anticipate this and try to catch you in a natural bottleneck.

Your silhouette is a give-away. Keep off ridges and backgrounds that may show you up. Break your profile using vegetation and smear your face with mud or berry juice. Pursuers are trained for look for unfamiliar shapes in the undergrowth so the more you blend in, the better.

CHOOSING A HIDE

Remember the BLISS formula when selecting a location for your hide and building it.

Blend. Make sure it doesn't stand out.

Low. Make sure the silhouette doesn't intrude on the view.

Irregular. Follow nature and avoid straight lines.

Small. The less impact on the environment, the less chance there is of being spotted.

Secluded. Reduce chances of being found by hiding up where people try not to go – in Belize I stood for half a day in a sewage-filled swamp because I knew that the hunter force would not spend as much time checking it as more salubrious surroundings. It's simple psychology, but it works.

Don't be tempted to use old buildings, however run-down they are. They're the first place your pursuers will look and you might find other people using them too. Thick, impenetrable vegetation makes for good cover, provided you don't disturb it when getting in and out.

If you're building a hide, dig it out of the ground. It's got to be deep and wide enough to take your body, any equipment you have and primitive provision for urinating and defecating. You should be using plastic bags for this to mask the smell, or burying it deep. Cover the trench with roofing, then replace the topsoil or turf as you found it.

In the Regiment we used to practise this in farmland – three of us holed up, living off the land and making sure we were not spotted. With a good hide, people can come walking past within a few feet, completely oblivious to the fact that there's an SAS unit close enough to reach out and touch them.

HIDING OUT

Don't stay more than 24 hours in the same hide and only move when it's dark. When you're holed up, use the time constructively either resting or planning. Don't forget to collect any earthworms or insects that come visiting for your next meal.

When you're moving between hides, use your time constructively gathering any food you can, looking for water and checking any snares or fish traps you may have set up.

Move carefully, especially near water and be sure to place traps out of sight on land and underwater in rivers. At the water source, the ground may well be soft and take a print easily, so watch where you stand and use fallen logs and/or rocks where possible.

URBAN ANTI-SURVEILLANCE

If you need to go to ground, you have two choices: find a lying-up position somewhere remote, or hide in plain sight – in the city.

CITIES

If you've gone to ground in a city, your appearance is your camouflage. Adapt it to local conditions, or if you can't change your appearance, stay in areas where you blend in.

Humans take in a lot of information subliminally and tend to fix on details that jar. It's your job to eradicate these details, so look at the things that may give you away: shoes, watch, jacket … anything that inspires envy or attention should be ditched. Moderate your body language to make yourself unthreatening and unobtrusive. You want to be the person that no one can be bothered to waste a second look at.

Orientate yourself by learning large, permanent landmarks. How does the city lie in relation to mountains, various skyscrapers or major roads? This can help you if you're lost – or if you want to get lost.

If you're staying in a hotel, familiarize yourself with the various exits and exit routes. When you go out, leave your TV on and a 'do not disturb' notice on the doorknob. Apart from anything else, it might put a burglar off.

As a general rule, don't open the door if room service arrives with something you haven't ordered.

IF YOU THINK YOU'RE BEING FOLLOWED

A good surveillance team should be able to follow even a wary target without being 'made'. That makes professionals who live or go undercover naturally suspicious, not to say paranoid. Anti-surveillance is not just about spotting your tail; it's also about building actions into your pattern of behaviour to put people off your scent or keep them at a distance.

ON FOOT

If you think you're being followed, you first have to work out who is following you. If you think they are dangerous, you'll need to do this without them noticing.

Make for underground stations if possible – communications equipment may not work in the tunnels. On a busy street, vary your speed, walk into department stores and out of them by different doorways.

In an urban environment, jump into a taxi if you can find one, and check the back window for activity on the street. Don't stay in too long, however and cover tracks when you disembark. Your taxi driver may be picked up and interviewed later.

By stopping dead opposite a window or some other reflective surface, you may be able to spot someone in the crowd change their behaviour. Watch their eyes. Your trackers will be looking at you when your back is turned, although they'll be sure to look away when you turn around. Incidentally, this was the reason the SAS took out the IRA team in Gibraltar back in 1988. The SAS guys were spotted when one of the IRA men looked around and saw one of them staring at him. He made a hand movement that the guys interpreted as a threat and so they dropped the three of them.

Doubling back is simple yet effective. If your follower is not part of a team, they will have to turn back too. Time your move carefully – if you double back and then get into a shop with multiple exits, you have a good chance of shaking off your pursuer.

By changing something noticeable about your appearance – a jacket or hat for example – you may throw a second pursuer off the trail, who will be relying on your clothes to 'make' you.

In Northern Ireland, targets had a number of anti-surveillance techniques. In the early days of the troubles, allegedly all they had to do was stop suddenly in the street, point and shout; 'I know you're following me.' Anyone not following would look surprised, or ask them what they were on about. Anyone who *was* following them would walk away quickly. Later, if a target thought they had seen their tracker, they would just stop them and ask the time. The trick was to get us to talk because accent is such a giveaway.

If you think you are being followed by a professional outfit, watch for small movements that will show they are talking into a cuff or lapel-mounted microphones. Ear-pieces for radios are now small and discreet, but are visible.

BY CAR

If you are in a car, going twice round a roundabout works well for throwing an attacker off your trail. They cannot follow you without making it obvious and you have a choice of exits to take. Stopping unexpectedly on the hard shoulder of a motorway is another good trick – no one can stop without your seeing who it is. It's a favourite meeting place for the Russian mafia and has the added advantage of road noise to mess up recordings.

BRIBERY AND CORRUPTION

As a last word, there may be times when offering money is your only option for getting out of a tight squeeze. In my experience there is a sort of etiquette that has to be gone through.

A sign that negotiations may be about to be opened is when the official or person you are dealing with tells you how complicated your situation is and how hard it might be to get out of it. You then say that you are keen to help in any way you can. He then says that he might know someone who can help – or he can –but it will involve a great deal of work/effort/risk.

Ask what the best of way is of securing this service. Make it clear that you have a need and are prepared to do what you have to do in order to fulfil it.

If money is wanted, you will find out how much very soon after this. After that, it's up to you to handle the situation. The difference between bribery and buying a service openly is subtle. With a service, it is clear what you are paying for. In bribery, you may have to go through a rigmarole to establish that there is a service to be offered, even if you are not sure what that service is.

Do not offer money unless you are certain it is wanted. It will get you into worse trouble.